Question-based
Bible Study Guide

When the Game Is Over, It All Goes Back In the Box

Good Questions
Have Groups Talking

By Josh Hunt

Contents

When the Game is Over, Lesson #1
Chapters 1 – 2; Learn Rule #1
Be Rich Toward God
Good Questions Have Groups Talking
www.joshhunt.com

Email your people and invite them to read chapters 1 – 2 of *When the Game Is Over, It All Goes Back Into the Box.* An informed group makes for interesting discussion.

OPEN:

Did you play Monopoly growing up? What is Ortberg's Rule #1? What can we learn from playing Monopoly?

DIG

1. **Luke 12.16 – 21. What did this man not learn from playing monopoly?**

   He seemed to be a decent fellow, this wealthy farmer. Sharp enough to turn a profit, savvy enough to enjoy a windfall. For all we know he made his fortune honestly. No mention is made of exploitation or embezzlement. He put his God-given talent to making talents and succeeded. Flush with success, he resolved to learn a lesson from the fable of the ant and the grasshopper.

The grasshopper, you'll remember, wondered why the ant worked so hard in the summer day. "Why not come and chat with me instead of toiling in that way?" The ant explained his labor: "I'm helping to lay up food for the winter and recommend you do the same." But the grasshopper preferred to flitter than work. So while the ant prepared, the grasshopper played. And when winter brought its harsh winds and barren fields, the ant nibbled on corn while the grasshopper stood on the street corner holding a cardboard sign: "Any work will do. I'll hop right to it."

The tycoon in Jesus' story wasn't about to play the role of the grasshopper. No food lines or soup kitchens for him. And no food lines or soup kitchens for us either. We empathize with the fecund farmer. Truth be told, we want to learn from his success. Has he written a book (Bigger Barns for Retirement)? Does he conduct seminars ("Recession-Proof Your Barn in Twelve Easy Steps")? Doesn't the barn stuffer model responsible planning? And yet Jesus crowns him with the pointy hat of the dunce. — Max Lucado, *Fearless: Imagine Your Life without Fear* (Nashville: Thomas Nelson, 2012).

2. **What do we learn about Christian living from this (negative) example?**

This rich man indwelled a one-room house of mirrors. He looked north, south, east, and west and saw the same individual—himself. I. I. My. I. I. My. I. My. My. I. My. No they. No thee. Just me. Even when he said you, he spoke to himself. "You have many goods. Take your ease."

And so he did. He successfully hoarded enough stuff so he could wine, dine, and recline. He moved to Scottsdale, bought a five-bedroom split-level on the third fairway of the country club. He unpacked the moving vans, set up his bank accounts, pulled on his swimming trunks, and dove into the backyard pool. Too bad he forgot to fill it with water. He popped his skull on the concrete and woke up in the presence of God, who was anything but impressed with his portfolio. "Fool! This night your soul will be required of you; then whose will those things be which you have provided?" (v. 20).

The rich fool went to the wrong person ("He thought to himself ") and asked the wrong question ("What shall I do?"). His error was not that he planned but rather that his plans didn't include God. Jesus criticized not the man's affluence but his arrogance, not the presence of personal goals but the absence of God in those goals. What if he'd taken his money to the right person (God) with the right question ("What do you want me to do?")? — Max Lucado, *Fearless: Imagine Your Life without Fear* (Nashville: Thomas Nelson, 2012).

3. What drove this man to hoard?

Accumulation of wealth is a popular defense against fear. Since we fear losing our jobs, health care, or retirement benefits, we amass possessions, thinking the more we have, the safer we are. The same insecurity motivated Babel's tower builders. The nations that spread out after Noah's flood decided to circle their wagons. "Come, let us build ourselves a city, and a tower whose top is in the heavens; let us make a name for ourselves, lest we be scattered abroad over the face of the whole earth" (Gen. 11:4).

Do you detect the fear in those words? The people feared being scattered and separated. Yet rather than turn to God, they turned to stuff. They accumulated and stacked. They collected and built. News of their efforts would reach the heavens and keep their enemies at a distance. The city motto of Babel was this: "The more you hoard, the safer you are." So they hoarded. They heaped stones and mortar and bricks and mutual funds and IRAs and savings accounts. They stockpiled pensions, possessions, and property. Their tower of stuff grew so tall they got neck aches looking at it.

"We are safe!" they announced at the ribbon-cutting ceremony.

"No you aren't," God corrected. And the Babel-builders began to babble. The city of one language became the glossolalia of the United Nations minus the interpreters. Doesn't God invoke identical correction today? We engineer stock and investment levies, take cover behind the hedge of hedge funds. We trust annuities and pensions to the point that balance statements determine our mood levels. But then come the Katrina-level recessions and downturns, and the confusion begins all over again. — Max Lucado, *Fearless: Imagine Your Life without Fear* (Nashville: Thomas Nelson, 2012).

4. The man was afraid, and he acted stupid. How can fear make us stupid?

During the economic collapse of October 2008, a Stamford, Connecticut, man threatened to blow up a bank. When he lost $500,000 of his $2,000,000 portfolio, he planned to bring a gun into the facility and take the lives of innocent people if necessary.[1] As if a shooting spree would do anything to restore his loss. Fear has never been famous for its logic.

If there were no God, stuff-trusting would be the only appropriate response to an uncertain future. But there is a God. And this God does not want his children to trust money. He responded to the folly of the rich man with a flurry of "Do not worry" appeals. "Do not worry about your life. . . . Do not seek what you should eat or what you should drink, nor have an anxious mind" (vv. 22, 29).

Don't follow the path of the wealthy bumpkin who was high on financial cents but impoverished of spiritual sense. Instead, "Do not fear, little flock, for it is your Father's good pleasure to give you the kingdom" (v. 32). This is the only occasion when Jesus calls us his "little flock." The discussion of provision prompts such pastoral concern. — Max Lucado, *Fearless: Imagine Your Life without Fear* (Nashville: Thomas Nelson, 2012).

5. What did this man desperately need to know about God?

I once rode on horseback with a shepherdess through the Black Mountains of Wales. The green valleys were cotton-puffed with heads of sheep. We came upon one member of the flock that had gotten herself into quite a fix. She was stuck on her back in the rut of a dirt road and couldn't stand up.

When the shepherdess saw her, she dismounted from her horse, looked at me, and chuckled. "They aren't the brightest of beasts." She righted the animal, and off it ran.

We aren't the brightest of beasts either. Yet we have a shepherd who will get us back on our feet. Like a good shepherd, he will not let us go unclothed or unfed. "I have never seen the godly abandoned or their children begging for bread" (Ps. 37:25 NLT). What a welcome reminder! When homes foreclose or pensions evaporate, we need a shepherd. In Christ we have one. And his "good pleasure [is] to give you the kingdom."

Giving characterizes God's creation. From the first page of Scripture, he is presented as a philanthropic creator. He produces in pluralities: stars, plants, birds, and animals. Every gift arrives in bulk, multiples, and medleys. God begets Adam and Eve into a "liturgy of abundance"2 and tells them to follow suit: "be fruitful and multiply" (Gen. 1:28).

Scrooge didn't create the world; God did.

Psalm 104 celebrates this lavish creation with twenty-three verses of itemized blessings: the heavens and the earth, the waters and streams and trees and birds and goats and wine and oil and bread and people and lions. God is the source of "innumerable teeming things, living things both small and great. . . . These all wait for You, that You may give them their food in due season" (vv. 25, 27).

And he does. God is the great giver. The great provider. The fount of every blessing. Absolutely generous and utterly dependable. The resounding and recurring message of Scripture is clear: God owns it all. God shares it all. Trust him, not stuff! — Max Lucado, *Fearless: Imagine Your Life without Fear* (Nashville: Thomas Nelson, 2012).

6. Why does Jesus call this man a fool? What do we learn about God from this?

If you're running to win, but you have only earthly goals in mind, your victory will be short-lived. It will be a withering type of thing. You have to have spiritual goals in mind. Things do get in the way of being excellent— things like pride and self-centeredness—but you have to try to keep those types of thoughts out. You have to do everything as unto the Lord, understanding what's spiritual and what's long-lasting.

I'm reminded of the Scripture passage about the guy who had the barns, was very blessed, and said he was going to build bigger barns to store all of his wares. God said to him, "You're a fool, because all these things will be taken from you this very night."

Where is your soul? That's the thing that's going to last. Our priorities are misguided if we think only in terms of individual excellence. Everything has to balance out. Excellence without service, or excellence without teamwork, is excellence for only your purpose. God has bigger and better things in store for you. —Tony Dungy / Fellowship Of Christian Athletes, *Heart of an Athlete Playbook: Daily Devotions for Peak Performance* (Grand Rapids, MI: Revell, 2012).

7. Does this hint that saving is a bad thing?

Being prudent and saving for a rainy day are good things. In fact, they're things that are encouraged in a number of different places in the Bible. But like any good thing, this strategy can be pushed too far. At what point does being smart and saving for the future turn into selfishness? What is the proper balance between saving and giving? — Mike Slaughter and Matthew L. Kelley, *First - Devotional: Putting God First in Living and Giving* (Nashville: Abingdon Press, 2013).

8. How much saving is too much?

Though there is no hard-and-fast answer, Jesus told a story that gives us guidance. A landowner had an excellent harvest. The harvest was so plentiful that he didn't have enough room to store it all! So he decided to build bigger barns to store his crop so he could survive on the surplus for several years.

This seems like a smart decision, right? But Jesus said that God was upset with the man, because if he died that night, all of his surplus would go to waste. The parable probably sounded strange to a first-century audience, and it sounds even stranger today. The man should have been a hero, right? He had every right to make a profit from his plentiful harvest. What exactly did he do wrong?

Verse 19 provides a clue. When the landowner was making these plans, he decided to rest on his laurels: "I'll say to myself, you have stored up plenty of goods, enough for several years. Take it easy! Eat, drink, and enjoy yourself!" But the plentiful harvest had given him far more than he needed, so he had the chance to do some incredible things with it. He squandered the chance, opting instead to celebrate, because he thought he had earned it.

What would have happened if, instead of storing up the surplus, the man had imagined possibilities for sharing the blessing? He could have put some of the crop aside to have good seeds for the following season. He could have taken the profits from selling those extra crops and given ten percent or more to the work of God. That would have been a good start.

But what should the man have done then? He was wealthy, comfortable, and successful, so we can assume he was used to setting goals and working toward them. What would have come next? One possibility would have been to reward those who had helped produce the bountiful harvest. After all, there was no way he could reap such a big crop all by himself. He had laborers to do the work in the fields. He could reward them for their good work with a nice bonus. He could also look around his community and see who was struggling to make it

from one day to the next. He might realize that he had
an opportunity to make their lives easier through a
generous gift. — Mike Slaughter and Matthew L. Kelley,
First - Devotional: Putting God First in Living and Giving
(Nashville: Abingdon Press, 2013).

9. **Eat, drink, and be merry, for tomorrow you die.
What is wrong with this life-strategy?**

At the end of the day, the man would only get so much
satisfaction out of eating, drinking, and taking it easy. He
will get hungry again and might have a hangover from
too much partying. The satisfaction he would get from
sharing his bountiful harvest would last far longer than
the enjoyment of a good meal and a nice bottle of wine.
He might sleep more soundly, knowing he had made
his neighbors' lives easier and that God had used him
to make his corner of the world a better place. He could
be filled with joy, because his faith had led him to save
wisely and give generously, to be "rich toward God."

God, help me to know how much is enough. I want to
be rich toward you, not toward myself. Show me how to
share my blessings so that all your children will benefit
from the gifts you have given me. May I glorify you in
all that I do. Amen. — Mike Slaughter and Matthew L.
Kelley, *First - Devotional: Putting God First in Living and
Giving* (Nashville: Abingdon Press, 2013).

10. **Ecclesiastes 2.18ff. Why did Solomon—the richest
man in the world at the time—hate all things?**

Solomon was born wealthy, and great wealth came to
him because he was the king. But he was looking at life
"under the sun" and speaking for the common people.
The day would come when Solomon would die and leave
everything to his successor. This reminds us of our Lord's
warning in the parable of the rich fool (Luke 12:13–21)

and Paul's words in 1 Timothy 6:7–10. A Jewish proverb says, "There are no pockets in shrouds."

A writer in the Wall Street Journal called money an article that may be used as a universal passport to everywhere except heaven and as a universal provider of everything except happiness.

Of course, you and I are stewards of our wealth; God is the Provider (Deut. 8:18) and the Owner, and we have the privilege of enjoying it and using it for His glory. One day we will have to give an account of what we have done with His generous gifts. While we cannot take wealth with us when we die, we can send it ahead as we use it today according to God's will (Matt. 6:19–34; 1 Tim. 6:17–19). — Warren W. Wiersbe, *Pause for Power: A 365-Day Journey through the Scriptures* (Colorado Springs, CO: David C. Cook, 2010).

11. Ecclesiastes 2.20. My heart began to despair. Why is he so blue?

But in the end he concludes that work cannot, all by itself, deliver a meaningful life. "So I hated life, because the work that is done under the sun was grievous to me. All of it is meaningless, a chasing after the wind" (Ecclesiastes 2:17). Why does he draw this conclusion?

When we work, we want to make an impact. That can mean getting personal recognition for our work, or making a difference in our field, or doing something to make the world a better place. Nothing is more satisfying than a sense that through our work we have accomplished some lasting achievement. But the Philosopher startles us by arguing that even if you are one of the few people who breaks through and accomplishes all you hope for, it's all for nothing, for in the end there are no lasting achievements. "I hated all the things I had toiled for under the sun, because I must leave them to the one who comes after me. And who knows whether that person will be wise or foolish? Yet they will have control over all the fruit of my toil into which I have poured my effort and skill under the sun. This too is meaningless. So my heart began to despair over all my toilsome labor under the sun" (Ecclesiastes 2:18–20).

Whether quickly or slowly, all the results of our toil will be wiped away by history. The person who takes the business after you, or who picks up the cause or organization after you, may undo all you have done. Of course, some history makers have brought inventions or innovations that stay with the human race for a long time, but those persons are very rare, and of course eventually even the most famous "will not be long remembered" (Ecclesiastes 2:16) since everything and every accomplishment under the sun will be ground to dust in the end—even civilization itself. All work, even the most historic, will eventually be forgotten and its impact totally neutralized (1:3–11).

In short, even if your work is not fruitless, it is ultimately pointless if life "under the sun" is all there is. — Timothy Keller and Katherine Leary Alsdorf, *Every Good Endeavor: Connecting Your Work to God's Work* (New York: Dutton, 2012), 100–102.

12. Back to Luke 12.16 – 21. Last verse. What exactly does it mean to be "rich toward God."

What does God, who has everything, need from us? Nothing, really. He reminds us in Psalm 50:12, "The world is Mine, and all its fullness." So, what does Luke 12:21 mean when it suggests that we should be "rich" toward God?

Paul tells us: "Let them do good, that they be rich in good works, ready to give, willing to share, storing up for themselves a good foundation for the time to come, that they may lay hold on eternal life" (1 Timothy 6:18-19).

The size of our bank balance doesn't determine our ability to be "rich" toward God. Whatever we have, we should recognize that it is God's and we are only stewards of it for a time. Good stewards in God's economy share their possessions with the church, the poor, the unfortunate, and the hungry.

True riches are found in giving, and God's Word says the giver will also be credited in heaven. — David Jeremiah, *Discovering God: 365 Daily Devotions* (Carol Stream, IL: Tyndale House Publishers, Inc., 2015).

13. T/F: "I feel rich!"

So what does it mean to be rich toward God? The Bible offers dozens of examples of heavenly or divine wealth, but let's just focus on a few. Here are some of the more obvious examples of what it means to be rich toward God.

Being rich toward God means having a relationship with him. When you become a Christian, you immediately become part of God's family. **That means that all the riches of heaven are yours. The Bible talks repeatedly about the inheritance that God's children have. As one of his kids, your eternal future is secure. You have wealth stored up that you can't even begin to measure or understand here on earth. You truly are rich.**

Imagine that you made some poor business and personal decisions and accumulated more than one million dollars of debt. That would be an overwhelming amount of debt to surmount, especially when you add in interest. Then imagine that a successful businessperson decided to help you out by paying off your debt, no strings attached. One day you're a million dollars in debt, the next you're totally debt free. How would you feel? Well, besides being extremely relieved, I imagine that you might also feel rich. Because of the benevolence of another person, you just saved over a million bucks!

That's what it means to be rich toward God. We were in debt to him. The cost of our sin was something we could never pay off. We could work for all eternity and never get out of debt to God. But in the moment that you yield your life to Jesus, in the instant that you cross the line from wanderer to worshiper, all your spiritual debts are forgiven. And not only that, but you also gain all the inheritance of a child of God. It's a spiritual rags-to-riches story, and there's no way for these riches to ever be lost.

The farmer in Jesus' story missed the point. You see, it doesn't matter how rich you are on earth; if you don't have a relationship with God, you're poor. —Will Davis Jr., *Enough: Finding More by Living with Less* (Grand Rapids, MI: Revell, 2012).

14. Years ago, Lowell Lundstrom wrote a song called, "A Rich Man Am I." (You might Google it to find the words.) What did he man "A rich man am I"?

Now if I were to put you in a barrel and put that barrel in the middle of the Mississippi River, where would you be? You'd be in the middle of the Mississippi River. If you're in Christ, and Christ is in the heavenlies, where are you? You're in the heavenlies also. "He hath raised us up together with Him," and we're seated with Him (Ephesians 2:6).

I got a letter from a friend a while back. And he didn't say, at the end of the letter, "Keep looking up." He said, "Keep looking down." That was good, because he said, "Adrian"—that's what he said. I knew what he meant. He said—"Adrian, you're seated with the Lord Jesus Christ in the heavenlies."

And so you know, Paul wrote this Book of Ephesians. You know where he was when he wrote the Book of Ephesians? He was in prison. But when you open the Book of Ephesians, you don't smell any prison air. You smell the breezes of Heaven. Paul, in prison, said, "Hey, I'm up in Glory. I am rich. I am rich in my person. I am accepted in the Beloved. I am rich in my position. I'm seated with Christ." — Adrian Rogers, "Christmas Is Spelled G-R-A-C-E," in *Adrian Rogers Sermon Archive* (Signal Hill, CA: Rogers Family Trust, 2017), 2 Co 8:9.

15. Is it possible to be rich and live like a poor person?

John G. Wendel and his sisters were some of the most miserly people of all time. Although they had received a huge inheritance from their parents, they spent very little of it and did all they could to keep their wealth for themselves.

John was able to influence five of his six sisters never to marry, and they lived in the same house in New York City for 50 years. When the last sister died in 1931, her estate was valued at more than $100 million. Her only dress was one that she had made herself, and she had worn it for 25 years.

The Wendels had such a compulsion to hold on to their possessions that they lived like paupers. Even worse, they were like the kind of person Jesus referred to "who lays up treasure for himself, and is not rich toward God" (Luke 12:21). — Daily Walk, June 2, 1993 / Galaxie

Software, *10,000 Sermon Illustrations* (Biblical Studies Press, 2002).

16. How is the life of the one who is rich toward God different—and better—than the life of the one who is not?

Being rich toward God means that you're eternally, not temporally, focused. After Jesus offered this parable, he chimed in on the not-so-sacred-art of worrying:

> Therefore I tell you, do not worry about your life, what you will eat; or about your body, what you will wear. Life is more than food, and the body more than clothes. Consider the ravens: They do not sow or reap, they have no storeroom or barn; yet God feeds them. And how much more valuable you are than birds! Who of you by worrying can add a single hour to his life? Since you cannot do this very little thing, why do you worry about the rest?

> Consider how the lilies grow. They do not labor or spin. Yet I tell you, not even Solomon in all his splendor was dressed like one of these. If that is how God clothes the grass of the field, which is here today, and tomorrow is thrown into the fire, how much more will he clothe you, O you of little faith! And do not set your heart on what you will eat or drink; do not worry about it. For the pagan world runs after all such things, and your Father knows that you need them. But seek his kingdom, and these things will be given to you as well. (Luke 12:22–31)

Folks who are always fretting about stuff down here can never be rich toward God. All that worrying and stressing never does any good; besides, God has already gladly given us all the wealth and authority of his kingdom. What are we worried about? People who are rich toward God don't get too wrapped up in the details of the here and now. They're looking ahead, up over the horizon, to the better life that awaits them. — Will Davis Jr., *Enough: Finding More by Living with Less* (Grand Rapids, MI: Revell, 2012).

17. How do we move toward becoming rich toward God?

To start with, we must decide we are going to do this. We must make our minds up that we will disentangle ourselves from the suffocating weight that comes with living an overly consumptive lifestyle. We make a choice to break free in order to live redemptively. This requires an honest evaluation of the differences between our needs and wants and how we use what we have for redemptive purposes. We must decide whether we would prefer to gather treasures for earthly living or invest in heavenly treasure, being rich toward God. And a hint for where to lay up heavenly treasure is to recognize that the only things that will last forever are not even things; they are people. So if we desire to lay up treasures in heaven, we need to look to how we can affect the lives of others.

My wife and I are continually amazed as we watch television shows that track people's searches for a new house. Time and time again the pursuit of a larger house comes about as couples discover they have a first or second child on the way. In many cases the house they live in is quite large, but the default mode is, "We have a child on the way ... we need more space." It's as if the pregnancy test included drinking some wacked-out "you need more space" Kool-aid.

Over the last half-century, Americans have been conditioned to believe that they need larger and larger houses. The first Levittown subdivision homes following

World War II contained 750 square feet. "By the '60s 1,100 square feet was typical, and by the '70s, 1,350. Now it's 2,469."3 Compare this to the average home size in the United Kingdom, which is just over 750 square feet. For some reason we have come to believe we must have more and more personal space. My best guess is that the desire for independence and privacy drives this.
— Alan Hirsch and Lance Ford, *Right Here, Right Now: Everyday Mission for Everyday People, The Shapevine Series* (Grand Rapids, MI: Baker Books, 2011), 144–145.

18. Summary. What do we learn about Christian living from the game of Monopoly?

When my daughter, Danae, was a teenager, she came home one day and said, "Hey, Dad! There's a great new game out. I think you'll like it. It's called Monopoly." I just smiled.

We gathered the family together and set up the board. It didn't take the kids long to figure out that old Dad had played this game before. I soon owned all the best properties, including Boardwalk and Park Place. I even had Baltic and Mediterranean. My kids were squirming, and I was loving every minute of it.

About midnight I foreclosed on the last property and did a little victory dance. My family wasn't impressed. They went to bed and made me put the game away. As I began putting all of my money back in the box, a very empty feeling came over me. Everything that I had accumulated was gone. The excitement over riches was just an illusion. And then it occurred to me, Hey, this isn't just the game of Monopoly that has caught my attention; this is the game of life. You sweat and strain to get ahead, but then one day, after a little chest pain or a wrong change of lanes on the freeway, the game ends.

It all goes back in the box. You leave this world just as naked as the day you came into it.

I once saw a bumper sticker that proclaimed, "He who dies with the most toys wins." That's wrong. It should say, "He who dies with the most toys dies anyway." — J. F. Dobson, Dr. *Dobson's Handbook of Family Advice: Encouragement and Practical Help for Your Home* (Eugene, OR: Harvest House, 2012).

19. **What is the take-away for you this week? What do you want to remember?**

20. **How can we pray for each other this week?**

When the Game is Over, Lesson #2
Chapters 3 - 4; Three Ways to Keep Score
Master the Inner Game
Good Questions Have Groups Talking
www.joshhunt.com

Email your people and invite them to read chapters 3 - 4 of *When the Game Is Over, It All Goes Back Into the Box.* You might mention something you found about the reading that was interesting. An informed group makes for interesting discussion.

OPEN:

How do you keep score at work? How do you know if you are winning or losing?

DIG

1. **Galatians 6.4 – 5. How do we know if we are winning or losing in our Christian walk?**

    The generality make out their righteousness by comparing themselves with some others whom they think worse. A woman of the town, who was dying of [sexually transmitted] disease in the Lock Hospital, was offended at a minister speaking to her as a sinner because she had never picked a pocket. — JOHN NEWTON / Elliot Ritzema, ed., *300 Quotations for Preachers* (Bellingham, WA: Lexham Press, 2012).

2. How is Christian living not like Monopoly this way?

It's all about getting ahead. You must prove your-self to be the best—whether it's through your intellect, beauty, wealth, or skills. People are naturally disposed to comparing themselves to others—to competing and seeking prominence at whatever they consider their strength.

But you don't have to put yourself through such a useless and destructive exercise. God loves you just the way you are. He's given you unique talents that he's going to work through, so you don't have to contend against other people—you can work with them.

Friend, don't compete. When God is working through you, you're already the best you can be. You're already a winner, so be gracious and act like it. — Baker Publishing Group, *Moments of Peace from the Psalms* (Grand Rapids, MI: Bethany House Publishers, 2007).

3. Without comparing ourselves to someone else. Why is comparison toxic?

Competition. Comparison. Corruption. These three habits are toxic, sticking a knife into cooperation, teamwork, companionship, and mutual growth. But you won't let the Toxic Cs bring you down! You are a bright light that shines in darkness! When others cannot see, you bring a smile. When others are unkind, you speak words of light and life. When you're around, the Toxic Cs disappear. You get rid of competition because you know who you are and refuse to compete. You dash comparison on the rocks of self-assurance. You take corruption and kick it out of your path.

Now it's time to reach out and help others see their own inner lights. Touch others with your light and watch as your dreams overtake you! — Gail M. Hayes, *One-Minute Success Secrets for Women* (Eugene, OR: Harvest House, 2012).

4. Who have you been tempted to compare yourself with? Has it made life better or worse?

There is one great error that people with both too-low and too-high self-esteem make. They are comparing themselves to others. God never calls us to compare ourselves with anyone! We each have been given a unique, one-of-a kind, irreplaceable purpose in God's plan. We have been created as we are by a loving God who desires for us to fulfill the purpose that He has for our lives. It is when we compare ourselves to others that we say, "I'm not like that person" and then conclude, "I'm not as good" or in some cases, "I'm so much better."

Comparison separates and divides us from one another, but of even greater consequence is the fact that comparison leads us to false conclusions about ourselves and, therefore, faulty behavior.

When we think we are better than others, we treat them as inferior, unworthy, or as failures. When we think we are not as good or valuable as others, we treat them with undue deference, resentment, frustration, and envy. Both sets of behavior keep us from loving others fully or appreciating the fullness of who God made them to be. — Charles F. Stanley, *Discovering Your Identity in Christ* (Nashville, TN: Thomas Nelson Publishers, 1999), viii.

5. We don't keep score in Christian discipleship by comparing ourselves to others. How do we keep score? How do we evaluate our progress in the faith?

Use this list as a spiritual checkup to evaluate your walk, and then let us know how we might pray for you.

Are you reading the Bible daily? If you adopted an annual reading plan at the beginning of 2014, is your reading up to date? If not, take time this week to caught up. You might choose, if necessary, to adjust your plan – but still read daily. If you did not adopt a plan in January, pick a strategy for rest of the year.

Are you praying daily? Are you praying regularly and recurrently (1 Thess. 5:17)? Do you pray for those in authority, including government and church leaders (1 Tim. 2:2)? Are you praying by name for other believers to speak the gospel boldly and clearly (Eph. 6:18-20, Col. 4:2-4)? Do you pray for your enemies (Matt. 5:44)?

How often have you shared the gospel this year? Is the gospel so striking to you that you cannot keep it to yourself? Have you reached beyond the church world to develop gospel-centered relationships with unbelievers? For what non-believers are you praying as Paul did (Rom. 10:1)? Ask God to increase your burden for lost people (Rom. 9:1-3) throughout the remainder of this year.

Are you faithfully fighting sin in your life? Be honest – have you experienced victory over sin this year? Is there a sin that continually haunts you even though you've sought to overcome it? If so, what steps do you still need to take this year? Confess that sin to someone? Seek accountability? Simply repent?

What scriptures have you memorized this year? Do you echo the desire of the psalmist: "May the words of my mouth and the meditation of my heart be acceptable to You" (Psalm 19:14)? Based on your memorization of God's Word this year, would I conclude that you treasure God's Word in your heart (Psalm 119:9-11)?

Are you serving faithfully in a local church? The church is much more than a place to attend; it is a family that loves us and provokes us to good works (Heb. 10:24). Through the first half of 2014, have you used your spiritual gifts as a member of a local body of Christ (1 Cor. 12:1-11, 1 Pet. 4:10)? Are you supporting His work financially? Commit today to invest yourself in God's church throughout the rest of 2014. https://thomrainer. com/2014/06/10-questions-six-month-spiritual-checkup/

6. **Philippians 2.5 – 7. Evaluation questions like the ones above can be helpful, but they can also miss the mark. If we are not careful, we will just turn into better behaved Pharisees. What is the goal of Christian living according to Philippians 2.5ff?**

We evaluate our walk not so much on the basis of how many Quiet Times we had as much as, "Are we becoming more like Christ?" Are we becoming more humble? More joyful? More content? More grateful? More loving? Less worried? Less anxious?

7. **This passage describes Jesus' humility. What is humility? How would you define it?**

Winston Churchill was famous for saying about a political opponent that he was as a humble man because he had much to be humble about. Humility comes to a person who grasps that all gifts, talents, opportunities, and accomplishments are from the hand of God. It is rare to hear a person take credit for all his or her accomplishments; even the most secular award recipients give God and others some credit.

Humility is the starting line for putting on Christ; its absence makes conforming to Christ impossible. God stands in opposition to any person who doesn't have it.10 Humility attracts God's grace, and just as surely, pride runs it off. I would define humility as the acknowledgement of who or what you are dependent on. Humility's power is that it frees a person to focus on others; it opens the door to begin to affect others as Christ did.

Jesus' attitude was one of humility, which comes from the Latin humus, which means earth or dirt. Philippians 2 testifies that Jesus took a humble position in that he became a human being. Because of his humility, Jesus was able to fit into the larger purpose of redemption. He did not cling to what so many of us think we need: recognition and the right to be treated with respect. Jesus was God, but he didn't insist on being treated as such. He lost his status as God, suffered at the hands of the people he came to help, and even felt abandoned by his Father.

It often takes a person who has endured tough times to communicate humility with power. People who have lost their health, money, or the limelight tell the most moving stories. When we lose our pride, lay aside our desire to control, decide to obey and live for others, humility becomes our habit. It makes its way into our character through the regular practice of prayer, through the assimilation of God's Word, and in living for others.
— Bill Hull, *Christlike: The Pursuit of Uncomplicated Obedience* (Colorado Springs, CO: NavPress, 2010), 85–86.

8. This passage describes Christ's submission. Paul says in Ephesians that we are to submit ourselves to one another. How are relationships better as we submit ourselves to one another?

Submission is motivated by love; any other force that can yield submission is limited. Forced submission does not feed the soul, nourish the spirit, or bring joy to one's life, which is why people who are freed from oppressive relationships in their families or businesses or even from criminal prosecution no longer submit to their oppressors. Jesus, however, modeled a submission that was fueled by love; therefore, it endured and had no limits. He submitted to his Father's will, which was for him to give up the privileges of divinity. There was no limit to Jesus' willingness to serve the Father he loved. The more he submitted to God's will, the more joy it brought him because he was pleasing the one he loved. That is the model of all human relationships, which is something we will consider later. For now, however, let it be said that submission is the fruit of humility. The two together form the identity of Jesus. When his disciples follow his example and submit to the Father out of love, their lives have a transformative effect on those they come in contact with. When a person submits and serves from a basis of love, that person is free from self-interest, and the joy comes through.

This truth is beautifully illustrated in the film Babette's Feast, which is based on a story by Isak Dinesen. It begins with a portrait of two spinsters, Martine and Phillipa, whose father is the leader of a strict religious sect. The sisters are tempted to leave the village and live the "life of sin," but in the end, both women settle down to assist their father. Over time the father dies and the sect doesn't produce joy, love, and acceptance. In fact, most of the relationships in the village are broken or damaged by slights, gossip, and misunderstandings. Babette is a former great chef in Paris who has moved to the sister's village. When she miraculously wins the lottery, she offers to prepare a meal for the sisters in honor of their father. People gather for the feast. When the guests sit down and begin to eat, they are impressed with the sauces. The taste of the food creates words of praise, indeed a sensual pleasure. The experience has power that melts the guest's defenses. As they enjoy the feast, their attitudes begin to soften and people begin to apologize. In one of the most poignant scenes, two women who have not spoken to each other for many years touch foreheads affectionately, saying, "God bless you." One woman begins to sing, and a man rises and quotes Psalm 85:10: "Unfailing love and truth have met together. Righteousness and peace have kissed." The story illustrates the healing of relationships, a rebirth of community. Babette loved people for their own sake. She used what she had: a little money and skill. Her act of love, based in humility, changed lives. — Bill Hull, *Christlike: The Pursuit of Uncomplicated Obedience* (Colorado Springs, CO: NavPress, 2010), 86–87.

9. **This passage describes Jesus's obedience to the father. Bonhoeffer said, "Faith is only real in obedience." What did he mean by that?**

Jesus' humble act of submission led to the only thing that mattered: obedience. Dietrich Bonhoeffer put it well when he said, "Faith is only real in obedience."11 Christian spirituality finds its only meaning in obedience. Any other destination for what we call our spiritual worldview would discredit it. The only road to a life of satisfying obedience is one paved with humility and submission. When the word obedience stands alone, it feels austere, possibly even legalistic. Jesus never thought of obedience as a sterile act of courage; it was his heart responding to his Father, another way of saying, "I love you." For him, obedience to the Father was uncomplicated and heartfelt. — Bill Hull, *Christlike: The Pursuit of Uncomplicated Obedience* (Colorado Springs, CO: NavPress, 2010), 87–88.

10. **Let's move on to chapter four. Before we do, who can summarize the message of chapter three?**

    Christian living is not competitive. We can all win. Winning is not so much about checking boxes as much as about being like Christ.

11. **2 Corinthians 4.16. What was the score in Paul's life at this point? Was he winning or losing?**

    It is easy in our world to lose touch with the value of the inward man. Because we are an accomplishment-oriented society, it is hard to "rank" the inward man on those scales that our culture deems important. Therefore, in order to feel significant, we focus on developing the outward things that give us credibility in the eyes of others.

    Paul said that the "outward man is perishing." No amount of working on it is going to change that. How sad it is to see people wanting to look youthful in their obituary picture in the paper when they are as dead as everyone else! But Paul had a different philosophy. He accepted the fact that the outward man is perishing and the inward man is going to live forever. — David Jeremiah, *David Jeremiah Morning and Evening Devotions: Holy Moments in the Presence of God* (Nashville: Thomas Nelson, 2017).

12. Outwardly, we are wasting away. What is that talking about?

So there is the outer man: that's the body. There's the inward man: that's the spirit. The outer man is perishing; it is dying. My friend, you, right now, are in a perishing condition. I don't want to be gruesome about it, but I want to tell you what you are doing this morning: You are dying; you are just sitting there, dying. All of us are dying a step at a time.

Think of life as a race, and you are being pursued by death. When you were a youngster, you started out, and you looked behind you, and there was a runner way back there. And you're just running along; you're not worried about him. He is so far behind; you don't worry about him at all. You're just running along fine in life's race. But, you know, when you get to be what some call middle age—and, by the way, that's always a strange term. You ask a 55-year-old man, "How old are you?" and he says, "Well, I'm middle-aged." How many 110-year-old men do you know?—but, anyway, when you get to be whatever we call middle age, and you're running along, and you look back, and that runner that was so far behind you, he's a lot closer now than he used to be. But that's all right; you're going along. And then, suddenly, your legs begin to get weak, and you're not running as you used to. And it seems like he is gaining strength. And you look behind you, and he's getting closer and closer and closer. And it seems like now, for every step you take, he takes two. And some can feel his breath on the back of your neck. Friend, I want to tell you, there's a runner behind you, and he's gaining on you every day. You may be young; you may be old—but he's going to catch you. He's behind you. — Adrian Rogers, "Your New House," in *Adrian Rogers Sermon*

Archive (Signal Hill, CA: Rogers Family Trust, 2017), 2 Co 4:16–5:8.

13. We are all growing old. What do we learn about growing old gracefully from this verse?

Scripture teaches us to number our days and to apply our hearts unto wisdom. It also says even though we're "wasting away" on the outside, we are being renewed inwardly day by day. Those two verses say a lot about the aging process. It's a lifelong journey that has neither a clear beginning nor clear ending. But there are signs along the way that one's body is changing. We see our hair turning gray. Wrinkles show up in our faces as they become seasoned and worn with time. We do things more slowly and deliberately. These are the signs of the outside wasting away.

But it's the inside that's being renewed daily. And that's what we want to concentrate on. This is the secret of happy aging. Although obvious signs of physical changes are known to all of us, life's journey takes us beyond the obvious. It reaches inside and teaches us lessons we can only learn with our mind, spirit, and heart. The outward appearance becomes secondary to a far more endearing beauty and strength. The physical appearance of youth may be gone, but the capacity to love, experience, enjoy, share, and create grow even stronger. Therefore, these are the areas we must learn to stop and ponder. —LUCI SWINDOLL (*Life! Celebrate It*) / Various Authors and Thomas Nelson Inc., *Patchwork Devotional: 365 Snippets of Inspiration, Joy, and Hope* (Nashville: Thomas Nelson, 2010).

14. Inwardly, we are being renewed. What is that talking about?

There is a pair of famous bronze gates in the city of Florence, which Michaelangelo, in a burst of admiration, declared were fit to be the gates of Paradise. They are panelled with noble figures and dainty pictures. Once they were gilded, and Dante referred to them as "The Golden Gates." But the centuries have worn off the gold—so that hardly a particle is left now. Still the fine masterly work of the artist abides in the solid bronze, looking none the less impressive in its severe simplicity. So while the years may wear away many meritorious accomplishments and much of the glitter of the natural life, the graces firmly ingrained in our soul by the Great Master of all Arts and Hearts will abide. No change can touch these, for "though our outward man perish, the inward man is renewed day to day" (2 Cor. 4:16). — AMG Bible Illustrations, *Bible Illustrations Series* (Chattanooga: AMG Publishers, 2000).

15. How can we be renewed day by day?

But how exactly do we demonstrate that we value the inward man? How do we invest in that part of us we know is most important? We have to go into the spiritual gymnasium and work out with the inward man just as we would work out with the outward man to build up muscles or lose weight.

Just as the outward body needs food, so the inward man needs food, and the Bible tells us that food is God's Word. — David Jeremiah, *David Jeremiah Morning and Evening Devotions: Holy Moments in the Presence of God* (Nashville: Thomas Nelson, 2017).

16. So, try really hard to be renewed. Is that what Paul is saying?

YOU ARE BEING RENEWED DAY BY DAY. SO DO
not be weighed down by yesterday's failures and
disappointments. Begin this day anew, seeking to please
Me and walk in My ways—focusing on today! As you do,
I am able to transform you little by little. This is a lifelong
process—a journey fraught with problems and pain. It
is also a journey full of Joy and Peace because I am with
you each step of the way.

Notice that you are being renewed. This is not
something you can do by your effort and willpower
alone. My Spirit is in charge of your renewal, and He
is alive within you—directing your growth in grace. Do
not be discouraged when you encounter problems and
pain along your way. These are vital parts of the renewal
process. Muster the courage to thank Me when you are
going through painful experiences. Find hope through
trusting that I continually hold you by your right hand—
and I am preparing you for Glory! — Sarah Young, *Jesus
Today: Experience Hope through His Presence* (Nashville:
Thomas Nelson, 2012).

17. Colossians 3.10 says we are renewed in knowledge. What is that talking about?

"The new man is being renewed unto knowledge."
However diligent our Bible study may be, there is no
true knowledge gained any farther than the spiritual
renewal is being experienced; "the renewal in the spirit
of the mind," in its life and inward being, alone brings
true Divine knowledge.

And what is now the pattern that will be revealed to this
spiritual knowledge which comes out of the renewal as
its true and only aim? The new man is being renewed

31

unto knowledge, AFTER THE IMAGE OF HIM THAT CREATED HIM Nothing less than the image, the likeness of God. That is the one aim of the Holy Spirit in His daily renewing; that must be the aim of the believer who seeks that renewing.

This was God's purpose in creation, "Let us make man in our image, after our likeness." How little the infinite glory of these words is considered. For nothing less than this, did God breathe His own life into man, that it might reproduce in man on earth a perfect likeness to God in heaven. In Christ, that image of God has been revealed and seen in human form. We have been predestined and redeemed and called, we are being taught and fitted by the Holy Spirit, to be conformed to the image of the Son, to be imitators of God, and to walk even as Christ walked. — Andrew Murray, *The Inner Chamber and the Inner Life* (New York; Chicago; Toronto; London; Edinburgh: Fleming H. Revell, 1905), 126–127.

18. Back up to Colossians 3.5ff. What do we learn about discipleship from these verses?

My definition of a disciple is this: One who meditates on the Word with a view to application in the power of the Holy Spirit. Every part is important:

1. We must meditate on the Word. We are transformed by the renewing of out mind. We must change our stinkin thinkin.

2. We must meditate with a view to application. We must become doers of the Word. We don't want to become smarter sinners.

3. We must operate in the power of the Holy Spirit. We must have a profound awareness that without Christ we can do nothing. And, we must have a profound

confidence that I can do all this through Him who strengthens me.

19. **What did you learn today? What do you want to think about some more? What do you want to apply? What small step could you take before end of day tomorrow?**

20. **How can we pray for each other this week?**

When the Game is Over, Lesson #3
Chapters 5 - 6; Untie Your Ropes / Resign as Master of the Board
Good Questions Have Groups Talking
www.joshhunt.com

OPEN:

Any runners in the room? When was the last time you ran?

DIG

1. **The title of Chapter 5 is "Untie the Ropes." Did you get a chance to read it? What does Ortberg mean, "Untie the Ropes"?**

    We must discard whatever will hold us down. We must discard the wrong priorities that keep us from what matters most. — John Ortberg, *When the Game Is Over, It All Goes Back in the Box* (Grand Rapids, MI: Zondervan, 2008).

2. **Hebrews 12.1. What do we learn about Christian living from this verse?**

    We behave differently when we know people are watching. We bite our tongues, hold our tempers, help meet a need, say the encouraging word, and even pray more circumspectly. This is why today's verse is a great follow-up to yesterday's lesson—if the departed saints are able to observe our actions, our talk quickly becomes our walk.

I know the Lord Jesus is always watching (and that fact alone is enough to keep me on the straight and narrow), but a different slant is added when I consider that my earthly father, who is now in heaven, may also be watching. It's something I remember when I'm alone. When I'm tempted to blurt out malicious remarks or do something over which I'd be embarrassed if I were found out, I stop. I'm surrounded by a great cloud of witnesses. A host of departed Old and New Testament saints, as well as Christian friends and family, are watching (and cheering me toward obedience). They are my witnesses, and this fact inoculates me against the temptation of foolish, private sins. — Joni Eareckson Tada, *More Precious than Silver: 366 Daily Devotional Readings* (Grand Rapids, MI: Zondervan, 2010).

3. How is the Christian life like a race?

Put on your running shoes—you're in a race! It's not a race measured by the clock, and it's not the daily race we sometimes run with overflowing schedule and commitments.

It's the race of all races—the one we started the day of our salvation. It's a race to be enjoyed, and one with our own personal trainer alongside.

While God calls us to run our best, He doesn't want us to carry fears or worries while running His course. He wants us to run with Him, full of joy, free of entanglements.

He hasn't left us clueless—we have His Word, which reveals the obstacles and is filled with the good news on how to run light. Jesus not only set us free from the penalty of our sins—but He also died to set us free from its power (Romans 6–8). What does that mean to us? It means we don't have to be captive to anything or anyone that would have an ungodly hold on us. — Fran Fernandez with Zondervan, *The Best Is yet to Come: 60 Devotions* (Grand Rapids, MI: Zondervan, 2009).

4. **Many times in Scripture Paul and others use sports metaphor—as is the case here. What can sports teach us about discipleship?**

In the Christian life, we have a handicap. If we are encircled by the greatness of the past, we are also encircled by the handicap of our own sin. No one would attempt to climb Mount Everest weighed down with a whole load of unnecessary baggage. If we want to travel far, we must travel light. There is in life an essential duty to discard things. There may be habits, pleasures, self-indulgences or associations which hold us back. We must shed them as athletes take off their tracksuits when they go to the starting blocks; and often we will need the help of Christ to enable us to do so. — William Barclay, *The Letter to the Hebrews, The New Daily Study Bible* (Louisville, KY; London: Westminster John Knox Press, 2002), 203.

5. **Notice it is a race "marked out for us." Do we all have the same race, or do we each have different races?**

Verse 1 concludes by telling us that God has marked out a race for us. He has laid out a course for our lives. There are places we are to go, things we are to do, challenges we are to confront. We do not know where this course winds on its way to heaven, nor, frankly, is it important for us to know. Our calling is to "run with endurance the race that is set before us" (Heb. 12:1). Many Christians spend far too much effort trying to figure out what lies ahead, when our calling is to persevere in faith wherever God should lead us. — Richard D. Phillips, *Hebrews*, ed.

Richard D. Phillips, Philip Graham Ryken, and Daniel M. Doriani, *Reformed Expository Commentary* (Phillipsburg, NJ: P&R Publishing, 2006), 530.

6. There are many right answers to this question: what is the application of this verse?

When you're driving by yourself, how do you respond when someone cuts you off? What do you do when you're in a hotel room with an array of cable channels at your fingertips? Perhaps no fact better deters us from sins done in secret than Hebrews 12:1. "Let us put aside the deeds of darkness and put on the armor of light. Let us behave decently, as in the daytime" (Rom. 13:12-13).

When I honor you in public today, Lord, help me to also remember to honor you in private. More than a great cloud of witnesses, I have you one day to answer to! — Joni Eareckson Tada, *More Precious than Silver: 366 Daily Devotional Readings* (Grand Rapids, MI: Zondervan, 2010).

7. "Throw off everything that hinders." What is that talking about?

There is an ad where a woman is walking down the street with a chain around her ankle, dragging a scale. With this I can identify. Every morning for years, the first thing I did was get on the scale; how my day began was determined by the number. Over time, God revealed my problem wasn't the scale, or the food—it was my being consumed with them.

However, when I looked to Jesus and not myself, He showed me that He came not only to save me from my sins but "to proclaim freedom for the captives [me and you] and release from darkness for the prisoners" (Isaiah 61:1).

I realized I had been set free from the tyranny of the scale. Then by faith in Him and His Word I began to walk it out. (I am still working on the eating part.) — Fran Fernandez with Zondervan, *The Best Is yet to Come: 60 Devotions* (Grand Rapids, MI: Zondervan, 2009).

8. **"…the sin that so easily entangles." Can think of an example of what this is talking about?**

When we turn to the matter of sin, the situation is far more serious. Hindrances weigh us down, but sin entangles our feet, possibly bringing us down to the ground. Notice how the writer puts it: "sin which clings so closely." The point is that sin entangles us. We take sin lightly at our great peril. Sin is deceitful, as we read in chapter 3, able to lead us off the path altogether. Therefore, we must be wise regarding sin, seeking grace from God to be free from actual sins that we know about, while shunning the temptations to sin that abound.

Think, for instance, how quickly and thoroughly a great man like King David fell into sin when he allowed his heart to lust after Bathsheba. How entangled he became, and what a horrible impact that sin had on his life and on his whole family, even the entire kingdom! He was running brilliantly, as almost no one had run before, but sin entangled him and took him down. Sexual sin and pride continue to entangle the feet of many today, including leaders in the church. — Richard D. Phillips, *Hebrews*, ed. Richard D. Phillips, Philip Graham Ryken, and Daniel M. Doriani, *Reformed Expository Commentary* (Phillipsburg, NJ: P&R Publishing, 2006), 532.

9. **Chapter 6: Resign as Master of the Board. What is the main message of this chapter?**

One of the strongest of myths is the illusion of control. "I am in control" is not just a lie; author Ernest Becker51 called this the vital lie because we need it for our egos to survive. "We don't want to admit that we are fundamentally dishonest about reality, that we do not control our lives, that we always rely on something that transcends us." He says that man will use the power of money, or a string of sexual conquests, or relationships with important people, or a prestigious job, or his ability to learn, to make him feel that "he controls his life52 and death ... he is a somebody—not just a trembling accident germinated on a hothouse planet that [Thomas] Carlyle for all time called a 'hall of doom.' "

But we are not in control. — John Ortberg, *When the Game Is Over, It All Goes Back in the Box* (Grand Rapids, MI: Zondervan, 2008).

10. **James 4.7 (Passion Translation) says, "Surrender to God." No big surprise here. Most of us are familiar with the concept from the old hymn, "I surrender all." Is life better or worse for those who live surrendered lives?**

There is no joy in life like the joy of sharing. Don't be content to have too much when millions in the world have too little. I should remember every time I read the Bible that millions have no Bible to read. We should bear in mind when we hear the gospel preached that more than half the world has never heard the gospel story. Let our lives, our means, and our prayers be shared with those millions who at this moment are wondering whether there is any relief from their distress.

Don't be a half-Christian. There are too many of such in the world already. The world has a profound respect for people who are sincere in their faith.

The Bible tells us that we can't serve God and mammon, that no man can serve two masters. Too many Christians, so called, are like the little chameleon which adapts its coloration to that of its surroundings. Even a critical world is quick to recognize a real Christian and just as quick to detect a counterfeit.

We must live surrendered lives. The Bible is explicit at this point. It says: "Know ye not, that to whom ye yield yourselves servants to obey, his servants ye are to whom ye obey; whether of sin unto death, or of obedience unto righteousness?" (Romans 6:16).

A friend of David Livingstone once said: "When I watched Livingstone carry out the 'leave all and follow me' life, I became a Christian in spite of myself." The world knows no greater challenge than the surrendered life. — Billy Graham, *The Secret of Happiness* (Nashville: Thomas Nelson, 2011).

11. As we study Scripture, we always want to study for application. How do we make living a surrendered life a reality in our lives?

When Jesus prayed His prayer of surrender, "Not My will, but Yours, be done" (Luke 22:42), He set the pattern for surrender for all who would follow Him into the kingdom of heaven....

But how do we accept Christ's terms of surrender, living daily on the cross? The only way I know is by beginning each day with a prayer of surrender: "Lord, today I surrender my life to You. I choose Your will to be done, not mine. I want to be closer to You, God, than

I am to myself. I accept Your terms for my life today and purpose to live personally the crucified life which I received position-ally through faith in Christ. I ask You to give me grace to be a surrendered soldier of the cross today. Amen." —DAVID JEREMIAH / Thomas Nelson, *A Daybook of Prayer: Meditations, Scriptures, and Prayers to Draw near to the Heart of God* (Nashville: Thomas Nelson, 2007).

12. What keeps us living surrendered lives?

We think we know best. We don't believe it is in our best interest to live surrendered lives. In the long run, we do what we really believe is best for us. If we believe that God is good and following Him is good and it is always in our best interest to live the Christian life, living a surrendered life becomes almost automatic.

13. Ephesians 5.21. Submitting to God may be easy compared to what we read in this verse. God is all-knowing, wise, good, loving and so forth. I get submitting to Him. How is life better for us when we live lives of submitting to each other?

The fifth chapter of Ephesians shows a clear connection between being continually filled with the Spirit and having a happy, fulfilling family life. Being filled with the Spirit means learning to submit to each other within the home, learning to say "I'm wrong" and "I'm sorry."

Father, I realize my need to be continually filled with Your Spirit. Empty me completely of "self-sins"— self-pity, self-confidence to the point of pride, self-centeredness—so that there is room for Your Spirit. I'm sick of ME, Lord...I need YOU! — Joy Jacobs, *They Were Women Too: Women of the Old Testament in Devotions for Today* (Chicago, IL: Wingspread, 1981).

14. Submitting to one another. Back up to Ephesians 5.18ff. What is the context of this command?

Now he's talking about the Spirit-filled life. And in the Spirit-filled life, there is a spirit of adoration and the spirit of accommodation. We praise God, and we submit to one another. If you're one of those individuals always talking about your rights, you're not Spirit-filled. A dead man has no rights. When you say, "I know my rights," you don't understand the New Testament. Submission is not merely for women; submission is one equal voluntarily placing himself under another equal, that Jesus Christ may be glorified. And so, don't have a spirit of arrogance, saying, "I'm not going to let somebody else tell me what to do. If it's not my way, I'm going to swell up like a poison pup." Learn to submit. Submit one to another. — Adrian Rogers, "Others," in *Adrian Rogers Sermon Archive* (Signal Hill, CA: Rogers Family Trust, 2017), Php 2:3–4.

15. Are wives to submit to husbands? Are husbands to submit to wives?

Now, here again is what we are to do. Not only are we to care for one another, but we are to submit to one another. Ephesians chapter 5, verses 18 through 21, tells us that we are to submit one to another. We are to submit one to another. I am to be submissive to you. I am the pastor of the church, but that doesn't mean I am the dictator of the church. Doesn't mean I am the boss of the church. If anybody's the boss, you are, the congregation. God, the Lord Jesus Christ, is the head of the church. The pastor is the leader of the church. The deacons are the servants of the church. The committees cause he church to function, but the same pleases the multitude and we're all in a mode of submission one to another. There are no big shots and no little shots. Don't get the idea that submission is for women. Women are to submit to their husbands, because the Bible commands it. Members are to submit to the pastor, because the Bible commands it. But, we're all to submit to one another. That's mutual submission. Submission is not just for women; it's for Christians. It's for those who love the Lord. — Adrian Rogers, "One Another: The Tie That Binds," *in Adrian Rogers Sermon Archive* (Signal Hill, CA: Rogers Family Trust, 2017), Jn 13:34.

16. There are two schools of thought on this, and might interest is that you understand both. It is my conviction that you don't really understand an issue until you can clearly state what the other side believes. The two sides in this case are complementarian and egalitarian. Let's start with the complementarian position. What do they believe and why?

In the complementarian viewpoint, God has given the husband a role of loving servant leadership. Reasonable complementarians believe that the Bible describes this role more as one of responsibility than privilege, however. The husband essentially becomes a living martyr in his commitment to and service for his wife (Eph. 5:25–33), and she becomes his helper. Part of the man's martyrdom is lovingly leading her. This is what many—myself included—believe the Bible teaches in Genesis 3:16, 1 Corinthians 11:3, Ephesians 5:22–32, Colossians 3:18–19, and 1 Timothy 2:12–14, among other passages, taken together and applied throughout the majority of the church's history until the previous generation or so.

This is a matter of scriptural interpretation, but as a side benefit, I believe that the complementarian view seems to square better with recent findings in neuroscience about how the male and female brains work, as well as what makes for successful relationships. I frankly think the Bible is pretty clear on this, though there are a growing number of scholars (which, in fairness, I do not claim to be) who disagree with me.

This isn't the place to convince you of the rightness or wrongness of either position. If you want to study it for yourself, just google "Wayne Grudem" for the complementarian perspective and "Gordon Fee" for the egalitarian one, and you'll get more than enough information.

As I said before, what matters more than whether you agree with me, Wayne Grudem, or Gordon Fee is whether you agree with each other. — Gary Thomas, *The Sacred Search: What If It's Not about Who You Marry, but Why?* (Colorado Springs, CO: David C Cook, 2013).

17. What is the egalitarian position?

Different views of gender roles are based on what theologians call "egalitarian" or "complementarian" views of marriage.

In general, the egalitarian viewpoint sees no such thing as gender roles in marriage. In this view, God doesn't call men to servant leadership; that's cultural conditioning more than it is scriptural. Every couple should make their own decisions about who does what best, divide up the responsibilities, and base their marriage on individual strengths and weaknesses. The husband isn't expected to be a leader but rather a fifty-fifty partner. The thought of him leading is, in itself, somewhat offensive and demeaning to his wife. Nobody has the final say, and neither partner has more responsibility than the other to provide, guide, and protect. Every verse that seems to suggest men have a leadership role at home or in the church can be explained away by context, later additions to the original manuscripts, a more refined study of the original language, or a "trajectory" view of Scripture that suggests the New Testament realized the first century wasn't ready for egalitarianism, so it simply laid the foundation for it in future generations. The fact that the church used to think that men needed to step up as leaders at home and in the church is a historical weakness that needs to be discarded and explained away, not a biblical truth to be applied today. — Gary Thomas, *The Sacred Search: What If It's Not about Who You Marry, but Why? (Colorado Springs*, CO: David C Cook, 2013).

18. Is this just an abstract, theological issue, or does it matter in the real world?

The problems with disagreement on this issue may not be what you think. Many wives in complementarian marriages still manage finances. Many such husbands do much or even all of the cooking, just as many egalitarian husbands can be strong leaders. This debate often gets muddled by superficial, nonbiblical issues that aren't concrete or even helpful. It's often sidetracked with silly stereotypes—as if all complementarian men are abusive chauvinist pigs and all egalitarian men are spineless effeminate liberals. The last thing I'd call Wayne Grudem is abusive (the guy left a prime teaching position at a prestigious school to go to a then no-name college in order to serve his wife's physical health). I've been a teaching assistant for Gordon Fee, and he is, I assure you, neither spineless nor effeminate nor wishy-washy when it comes to biblical authority.

Most of the common misconceptions about gender roles aren't at a biblical level. Who handles finances, who cleans and cooks, who chooses where to go on vacation, or even what will constitute 99.9 percent of the general household decisions—biblical gender roles don't usually speak to such issues. But the notion of gender roles does affect marital expectations, how to raise children, what church you will attend, and how one views Scripture, all of which matters deeply.

A woman who expects her husband to be a spiritual leader and yet marries a man who finds such a concept demeaning to women and therefore offensive is going to find herself in repeated unresolvable conflicts. When finances get tight, for instance, she might expect him to step it up and get a better-paying job. He might think, "Why don't I stay home and you get a second job?" If your husband doesn't even believe in spiritual leadership, you can't expect him to become a spiritual leader. If that's what you really want, at least marry a guy who has that mind-set.

Guys who feel called to lead in their home but aren't allowed to do so will feel emasculated. Women who want their guys to lead but marry guys who don't will feel frustrated. Women who strongly adhere to the egalitarian perspective but who marry complementarians may not feel respected and will have serious problems when it comes to how the children are raised.

In a mixed egalitarian/complementarian marriage, both the husband and wife will likely try to treat the other according to their perceived sense of marital duties, but those duties won't be received as such—they'll be resented. What a complementarian woman finds loving and respectful, an egalitarian woman might find demeaning and frustrating, and vice versa. Since this rises to the level of biblical application, it must be frustrating to the extreme to aspire toward something that your spouse finds offensive.

People who disagree on this issue can still worship the same God, but it will be difficult for them to raise the same kids or operate the same household. — Gary Thomas, *The Sacred Search: What If It's Not about Who You Marry, but Why?* (Colorado Springs, CO: David C Cook, 2013).

19. The bottom line is this. God calls all of us to live a "you-first" life rather than a "me-first" life. How would the world be a better place if we all lived "you-first" lives?

Ernest Gordon's surroundings looked bleak. Men huddled, shivering with tropical diseases. Gordon had lost track of how many had died from starvation, disease, overwork, or execution. One man, Dusty, was hanged on a tree to die like Jesus. Others just lost hope and passed away in their sleep.

He thought back on the past few months. Gordon had been a proud Scottish warrior helping defend the British outpost of Singapore at the outbreak of World War II. Then the Japanese attacked. Now he found himself captive in the infamous Chungkai prison camp, where "the rhythm of death obsessed us with its beat." 1

Then two remarkable things happened. First, word spread of a prisoner who, in the name of Jesus, offered his own food and stayed by the side of his bunkmate to nurse him back from the brink of death. His bunkmate survived, but he did not. Second, when a work detail was accused of stealing a shovel and its members were threatened with execution, one man stepped forward to "confess" to the theft to save the lives of the others. The enraged guard beat him, crushing his skull. A recount of the shovels showed none was missing.

What Gordon now saw defied explanation. In light of these sacrifices, the attitude in the camp quickly shifted from "me first" to "you first." Awakened from their self-pity, men changed one another's filthy bandages and even attended to the wounds of enemy soliders brought to the camp. The experience of death changed as prisoners stopped piling up bodies and instead elected chaplains to conduct funerals to honor the fallen. Life steadily regained meaning.

Restored to their humanity, the prisoners formed a library and taught courses in everything from math to philosophy to languages (nine of them). They staged plays. Having retrieved six violins from a relief shipment, they formed an orchestra and held concerts.

Camp conditions overall had not changed. Frightful diseases still claimed lives. Food was still scarce and nauseating. "Death was still with us—no doubt about that," wrote Gordon. "But we were slowly being freed from its destructive grip." 2 How these men were able to overcome the horrors of a POW camp offers deep insight into how a Christian worldview overcomes the idea viruses that multiply our suffering. Hurt will not win. Indeed, it has already lost. Here's how we know.
— Jeff Myers, *The Secret Battle of Ideas about God: Overcoming the Outbreak of Five Fatal Worldviews* (Colorado Springs, CO: David C. Cook, 2017).

20. What do you want to remember and apply from today's study?

21. How can we pray for each other this week?

When the Game is Over, Lesson #4
Chapters 7 – 9
No One Else Can Take Your Turn
Remember Your Stuff Isn't Yours
Prevent Regret
Good Questions Have Groups Talking
www.joshhunt.com

OPEN:

Have you ever bought anything you regretted buying?
Who has a story?

DIG

1. **Chapter 7. No One Else Can Take Your Turn. What is that about?**

    You are not a pawn, a victim of circumstances beyond your control. Instead, you are responsible for your own life. No one else can take your turn. There are no designated hitters. You are not allowed to say, "Pass." — John Ortberg, *When the Game Is Over, It All Goes Back in the Box* (Grand Rapids, MI: Zondervan, 2008).

2. Daniel 1.8. Let's look this up in a number of translations. Are you all familiar with how to do this using the YouVersion Bible app?

But Daniel **resolved** not to defile himself with the royal food and wine, and he asked the chief official for permission not to defile himself this way. Daniel 1:8 (NIV2011)

But Daniel **made up his mind** not to eat the food and wine given to them by the king. He asked the superintendent for permission to eat other things instead. Daniel 1:8 (TLB)

But Daniel **determined** that he would not defile himself by eating the king's food or drinking his wine, so he asked the head of the palace staff to exempt him from the royal diet. Daniel 1:8 (MSG)

But Daniel **purposed** in his heart that he would not defile himself with the portion of the king's meat, nor with the wine which he drank: therefore he requested of the prince of the eunuchs that he might not defile himself. Daniel 1:8 (KJV)

3. What do we learn about Christian living from this passage?

The Scriptures in fact have a quite thorough account of POWs and hostages who refused passivity.

Daniel in exile took control of his diet: "But Daniel resolved that he would not defile himself with the royal rations of food and wine."

Peter and the other apostles refused to accept a gag order against preaching the gospel as a Get-Out-of-Jail-Free Card.

Paul and Silas took control of their time by holding a sing-along: "About midnight Paul and Silas were praying and singing hymns to God, and the prisoners were listening to them"—as if the other prisoners had a choice!

Faith believes that with God, we are never helpless victims. — John Ortberg, *If You Want to Walk on Water, You've Got to Get out of the Boat* (Grand Rapids, MI: Zondervan, 2008).

4. Context. What is the rest of this story?

OBEDIENCE TO GOD BRINGS PHYSICAL AND SPIRITUAL STRENGTH

- Daniel made a commitment to obey God., v. 8

- God backed up Daniel's resolve with supernatural support., v. 9

- Daniel requested only vegetables and water for himself and his three companions for their meals for ten days., v. 12

- Daniel trusted in the faithful provision of his God., v. 13

- The four men became noticeably healthier and better nourished., v. 15

- They continued eating only vegetables as testimony to their unwavering commitment to obey God., v. 16

- God blessed Daniel and the other men with great knowledge and understanding., v. 17

- God further blessed Daniel with the ability to interpret dreams and visions., v. 17

- King Nebuchadnezzar considered the four men to be ten times wiser than anyone in his kingdom., v. 20

— June Hunt, *Biblical Counseling Keys on Overeating: Freedom from Food Fixation* (Dallas, TX: Hope For The Heart, 2008), 28–29.

5. Genesis 1.26. "Let them have dominion…" (ESV; KJV) What do we learn about ourselves from this? What is the application?

Man has a special status in creation because he is the only creature to have been made in the image of God (Genesis 1:26). One of the consequences of being made in the image of God is that mankind is made to have dominion over God's creation. This is described in Psalm 8: 'When I consider Your heavens, the work of Your fingers, the moon and the stars, which You have ordained, What is man that You are mindful of him? … You have made him to have dominion over the works of Your hands; You have put all things under his feet … O Lord, our Lord, how excellent is Your name in all the Earth!' (Psalm 8:3–9). — Stuart Burgess, *He Made the Stars Also: What the Bible Says about the Stars* (Epsom: Day One Publications, 2001), 142.

6. What do we learn about our work from this verse?

Amazingly enough, research shows that the best moments of our lives don't come from leisure or pleasure. They don't involve sex or chocolate. They come when we are totally immersed in a significant task that is challenging, yet matches up well to our highest abilities. In these moments, a person is so caught up in an activity that time somehow seems to be altered; their attention is fully focused, but without having to work at it. They are deeply aware without being self-conscious; they are being stretched and challenged, but without a sense of stress or worry. They have a sense of engagement or oneness with what they are doing.

This condition is called "flow," because people experiencing it often use the metaphor of feeling swept up by something outside themselves. Studies have been done over the past thirty years with hundreds of thousands of subjects to explore this phenomenon of flow. Ironically, people experience it far more in their work than they do in their leisure. In fact, the time of week when "flow" is at its lowest ebb in America is Sunday morning, because so many people do not know what they want to do. Sitting around does not produce flow.

I believe this picture of "flow" is actually a description of what the exercise of dominion was intended to look like. God says in Genesis that human beings are to "rule" over the earth, or to exercise "dominion." We often think of these words in terms of "dominating" or "bossing around." But the true idea behind them is that we are to invest our abilities to create value on the earth, to plant and build and write and organize and heal and invent in ways that bless people and make the earth flourish.

Draw a graph in which the vertical axis represents the strengths God has given you and the horizontal axis represents the challenge of the task before you. If your skill level is very high, but the challenge of the task is too low, you experience boredom. If your skill level is too low, and the challenge of the task is too high, you experience frustration and anxiety. But when the level of the challenge you face matches the level of the skills you possess — then you are set up for flow.

All skill is God-given, and we are invited to live in conscious interaction with the Spirit as we work, so that he can develop the skills he gives us. Work is a form of love. We cannot be fully human without creating value.

We do not work mainly for money, recognition, promotion, applause, or fame. We work for flow. We live for flow. We hunger for the experience of flow, and when it is present, something happens in our spirit as we connect with a reality beyond ourselves and partner with God. This is why the psalmist says, "Unless the Lord builds the house, those who build it labor in vain." Flow is part of what we experience in that partnership, and in that, God in turn uses flow to shape us. — John Ortberg, *The Me I Want to Be* (Grand Rapids, MI: Zondervan, 2009).

7. **Chapter 8: Remember Your Stuff Is Not Yours. What is the big idea of this chapter? Feel free to peek.**

It's only stuff. Houses and hotels are the crowning jewels in Monopoly. But the moment the game ends they go back in the box. So it is with all our stuff. — John Ortberg, *When the Game Is Over, It All Goes Back in the Box* (Grand Rapids, MI: Zondervan, 2008).

8. **Matthew 6.19 – 24. We always want to read the Bible for application. We want to be doers of the Word, not hearers only. We want to be disciples, not smarter sinners. What is the application of this passage?**

A man's treatment of money is the most decisive test of his character–how he makes it and how he spends it. — James Moffatt

If a person gets his attitude toward money straight, it will help straighten out almost every other area in his life. — Billy Graham

— John Ortberg, *Now What? God's Guide to Life for Graduates* (Grand Rapids, MI: Zondervan, 2011).

9. Agree or disagree: Money is God's #1 competitor.

It costs something when Jesus calls you.

I have a friend. He's a businessman. He's in his seventies now. But years ago, I attended his church one time on a Sunday when he gave a terrific message. We talked afterwards, and he said to me, "You know, when I was a young man, I always felt that I ought to go into pastoral ministry."

And I asked him, "Why didn't you?"

Well, when it came right down to it, it was just money. He was already into the business world, and he was doing quite well. So he didn't follow what he sensed was God's calling on his life.

Friends, I don't know how else to say this. It's only money. But people get all twisted up in knots over it, and they stay awake at night thinking about it, and they stew and they worry and they get anxious and they scheme and they trade away their integrity, only to get a little pile, a little more of it. And their hearts get all knotted up, and they worry that somebody else might get ahold of it. And they throw away their lives running after more of it.

But it's only money. It's never a reason not to follow Christ. It's never a reason not to do the thing that God needs you to do. It's only money.

When you work—whether you love it or whether it's not real thrilling to you—you ought to give it the best that you have when you're there. But don't give it time or energy or allegiance that keeps you from living in the way of Christ. It's not worth it. — John Ortberg, *Now What? God's Guide to Life for Graduates* (Grand Rapids, MI: Zondervan, 2011).

10. Store up treasures in Heaven. How exactly do you do that?

So the wisdom of Jesus is that we should "lay up for ourselves treasures in heaven" (6:20), where forces of nature and human evil cannot harm what we treasure. That is to say, direct your actions toward making a difference in the realm of spiritual substance sustained and governed by God. Invest your life in what God is doing, which cannot be lost.

Of course this means that we will invest in our relationship to Jesus himself, and through him to God. But beyond that, and in close union with it, we will devote ourselves to the good of other people—those around us within the range of our power to affect. These are among God's treasures. "The Lord's portion," we are told, "is his people" (Deut. 32:9). And that certainly includes ourselves, in a unique and fundamental way. We have the care of our own souls and lives in a way no one else does, and in a way we have the care of no one else.

And we also care for this astonishingly rich and beautiful physical realm, the earth itself, of which both we and our neighbors are parts. "You have established the earth and it continues. All things stand this day according to your directions. For all things are your servants" (Ps. 119:91). God himself loves the earth dearly and never takes his hands off it. And because he loves it and it is good, our care of it is also eternal work and a part of our eternal life. — Dallas Willard, *The Divine Conspiracy: Rediscovering Our Hidden Life in God* (Grand Rapids, MI: HarperCollins e-books, 2009).

11. 1 Timothy 6.10. What evil comes from loving money?

The apostle Paul also warns about the money monster: "For the love of money is a root of all kinds of evil. Some people, eager for money, have wandered from the faith and pierced themselves with many griefs" (1 Tim. 6:10).

God wants to fill our hearts and lives with riches beyond compare. The problem is, we hold so tightly to the toys and trinkets of this world that we miss the treasures God offers. The money monster is alive and well. It does not sleep or rest but is always looking for a way to get a grip on our hearts.

God has the power to break this creature's influence. Like a loving parent, God desires to give good gifts that bring joy and contentment to his children. It is time to receive the riches of heaven. The question is, Are we ready to trade the fakes, forgeries, and counterfeit treasures for the riches God offers us? — Kevin G. Harney, *Seismic Shifts* (Grand Rapids, MI: Zondervan, 2009).

12. Again, read for application. We know we ought to give our tithes and offerings. What are other applications of this verse?

I talked to a man waiting my table at a restaurant who is working two minimum-wage jobs. Not one, but two minimum-wage jobs, just to make ends meet and to support his mom. I wasn't going to do anything particularly generous. Then I remembered Jesus said, "Do not store up for yourselves treasures on earth. . . . But store up for yourselves treasures in heaven" (Matthew 6:19-20). This man's need became an open door for a small gesture, for a quick prayer. — John Ortberg, *All the Places to Go . . . How Will You Know?*

God Has Placed before You an Open Door. What Will You Do? (Carol Stream, IL: Tyndale House Publishers, Inc., 2015).

13. How is the Christian view of money different from the world?

The system of this world invites us to hoard everything we have for a rainy day. Or to spend it selfishly today because there might not be a chance to enjoy it tomorrow. When we live this way, we expose a heart in love with the stuff of this world. But a person with a heart captured by Jesus' grace declares war on a culture that is all about me, mine, and more. This kind of person raises a banner that says, "Other people matter, the world is bigger than my needs and wants, and God's interests and concerns are worth investing in." A generous giver sends a message that says, "God and his people live with a whole different economy. Our hearts are not bound by the love of material things. There are investments that earn more than earthly dividends." When our hearts beat with the heart of Jesus, generosity can't be stopped. — Kevin G. Harney, *Seismic Shifts* (Grand Rapids, MI: Zondervan, 2009).

14. How do we evaluate our progress as Christians? Is it how many times we attend church, or read our Bibles? How did Jesus answer this question?

How do we know whether our hearts are surrendered to God? Jesus says that we can look at where we store our treasure. If massive portions of our resources are stored away in bank accounts, spent on toys, and tied up in earthy things, the money monster just might have a tighter grip on our hearts than we know. On the other hand, if we are investing in eternal things, living with open hands, and growing in generosity, our hearts are resting safely in Jesus' hands. — Kevin G. Harney, *Seismic Shifts* (Grand Rapids, MI: Zondervan, 2009).

15. Chapter 9: Prevent Regret. What is the "Big Idea" of this chapter?

We need to ask ourselves what we are doing (or not doing) with our lives now that could lead to deep regret. Life always plays in a forward direction; it never goes backward. Once a move is made, there is no going back. — John Ortberg, *When the Game Is Over, It All Goes Back in the Box* (Grand Rapids, MI: Zondervan, 2008).

16. Can we take a moment to get vulnerable? What regrets do you live with?

I think of a man I know who had a strong concern about the problem of educational inequality. But he found he was unable to let go of his desire to make a lot of money in order to give time to that cause. His financial obsessions led to alienation from his family, and ironically, his investments turned out badly. He had to declare bankruptcy. Eventually this led him to go into teaching at a school in an underresourced area. His only regret is that it took him so long.

"If I Have Chosen the Wrong Door, I Have Missed 'God's Will for My Life' and Will Have to Settle for Second Best"

This is a form of what social scientists refer to as "counterfactual thinking," where people who don't like the outcome of one decision obsess over what might have happened in an alternative hypothetical scenario. The classic phrase is "If only . . ." "If only I'd taken that job/dated that person/chosen that school/made that investment instead of this one."

A businessperson comes to believe he should have been a pastor and lives with a chronic sense of guilt.

A woman believes she married the wrong man and fantasizes over an imaginary marriage to the man she now decides was God's Plan A.

We tend to do counterfactual thinking more often in a negative direction than a positive one. We think disproportionately about those outcomes that disappointed us and not the ones that filled us with gratitude that we could have missed out on. And the wrong kind of counterfactual thinking leads to paralysis, depression, self-pity, and stagnation. God is never calling us through that door.

Paul makes a helpful distinction for the church at Corinth. He says there is a "godly sorrow [that] brings repentance" and a "worldly sorrow [that] brings death" (2 Corinthians 7:10). The right kind of sorrow over a wrong decision always creates energy rather than despair. It enables us to learn from past mistakes and grow into great wisdom. Godly sorrow is filled with hope.

Worldly sorrow is energy depleting. In worldly sorrow we look at our wrong choices as though the world — rather than God —is our only hope. We live in self-pity and regret. We obsess over how much better our lives might have been had we chosen Door #1. — John Ortberg, *All the Places to Go . . . How Will You Know? God Has Placed before You an Open Door. What Will You Do?* (Carol Stream, IL: Tyndale House Publishers, Inc., 2015).

17. What are we to do with the regrets we live with?

Jesus did not say, "The Kingdom of God is at hand — regret and believe the Good News!" The difference between regret and repentance is the difference of an opened door to a new future.

God's doors, like his mercies, are new every morning.

Frederick Buechner writes, "The sad things that happened long ago will always remain part of who we are just as the glad and gracious things will too, but instead of being a burden of guilt, recrimination and regret that make us constantly stumble as we go, even the saddest things can become, once we have made peace with them, a source of wisdom and strength for the journey that still lies ahead."[29] — John Ortberg, *All the Places to Go . . . How Will You Know? God Has Placed before You an Open Door. What Will You Do?* (Carol Stream, IL: Tyndale House Publishers, Inc., 2015).

18. We are about out of time. How do we live lives without regret?

What is the best way to live without regret?

- Choose to live in such a way that you do your best in every task and in every relationship.

- Choose to trust God in every area of your life—every decision, every choice, every opportunity He sends your way.

- Choose to obey God. Keep His commandments.

- Choose to forgive others fully and freely.

- Choose to pursue what God reveals to you as His path for you to follow.

— Charles F. Stanley, *God's Way Day by Day* (Nashville, TN: Thomas Nelson Publishers, 2004), 115.

19. **What did you learn today? What do you want to remember and apply? What do you want to think about some more?**

20. **How can we pray for each other this week?**

When the Game is Over, Lesson #5
Chapters 10 - 11
Play by the Rules
Fill Each Square with What Matters Most
Good Questions Have Groups Talking
www.joshhunt.com

OPEN:

Would you say you are, by nature, a rule breaker, or a rule follower?

DIG

1. **Chapter 10. Play by the rules. Let's start with a little Google Bible Study. What verses can you find on the topic of integrity?**

   Proverbs 11:3 The integrity of the upright guides them, but the unfaithful are destroyed by their duplicity.

   Proverbs 28:6 Better the poor whose walk is blameless than the rich whose ways are perverse.

   1 Peter 3:16 keeping a clear conscience, so that those who speak maliciously against your good behavior in Christ may be ashamed of their slander.

Proverbs 12:22 The LORD detests lying lips, but he delights in people who are trustworthy.

Proverbs 21:3 To do what is right and just is more acceptable to the LORD than sacrifice.

2 Corinthians 8:21 For we are taking pains to do what is right, not only in the eyes of the Lord but also in the eyes of man.

Proverbs 4:25-27 Let your eyes look straight ahead; fix your gaze directly before you. 26 Give careful thought to the paths for your feet and be steadfast in all your ways. 27 Do not turn to the right or the left; keep your foot from evil.

Hebrews 13:18 Pray for us. We are sure that we have a clear conscience and desire to live honorably in every way.

Luke 6:31 Do to others as you would have them do to you.

https://www.biblestudytools.com/topical-verses/bible-verses-about-integrity/

2. What is integrity? How would you define it?

"Integrity" means "sound, complete, without blemish, crack, or defect." In the construction business, integrity is created by adhering to building codes that ensure the building will be properly designed to be safe and function according to its purpose. Webster's dictionary has a simple word for integrity: "honesty." — H. Norman Wright, *The One-Minute CounselorTM for Men: Practical Help for *avoiding Temon *improving Communication *loving Your Wife* (Eugene, OR: Harvest House, 2015).

3. What does integrity cost us?

"I'm no saint, but I want to take a stand for Jesus. How can I demonstrate my faith?"

This is a great goal! We need more men of integrity. "The one whose walk is blameless, who does what is righteous, who speaks the truth from their heart...will never be shaken" (Psalm 15:2,5). But integrity is a costly virtue. What are some of the costs? Time, effort, money, and perhaps even popularity and respect. Integrity isn't popular because it makes some people uncomfortable with their own ethics and decisions, especially in the business world. — H. Norman Wright, *The One-Minute CounselorTM for Men: Practical Help for *avoiding Temon *improving Communication *loving Your Wife* (Eugene, OR: Harvest House, 2015).

4. What does lack of integrity cost us?

"How will integrity make my life better? How will that draw people to Jesus?" you ask.

- Integrity helps you avoid problems. "The integrity of the upright guides them, but the unfaithful are destroyed by their duplicity" (Proverbs 11:3).

- Integrity gives you a solid footing. "The man of integrity walks securely, but he who takes crooked paths will be found out" (Proverbs 10:9).

- Integrity gives you something that lasts. "The days of the blameless are known to the LORD, and their inheritance will endure forever" (Psalm 37:18).

- Integrity provides a blessing for your children. "The righteous man leads a blameless life; blessed are his children after him" (Proverbs 20:7)...

- Integrity pleases God. "I know, my God, that you test the heart and are pleased with integrity" (1 Chronicles 29:17a).

- Integrity makes you more like Jesus. " 'Teacher,' they said, 'we know you are a man of integrity and that you teach the way of God in accordance with the truth...' " (Matthew 22:16b).8

Embrace integrity. It's a hallmark of a righteous man. — H. Norman Wright, *The One-Minute CounselorTM for Men: Practical Help for *avoiding Temon *improving Communication *loving Your Wife* (Eugene, OR: Harvest House, 2015).

5. How is life better for people of integrity?

I want to be ethical, and I believe that you do too. Furthermore, I know it really is possible to do what's right and succeed in business. In fact, according to the Ethics Resource Center in Washington, D.C., companies that are dedicated to doing the right thing, have a written commitment to social responsibility, and act on it consistently are more profitable than those who don't. James Burke, chairman of Johnson and Johnson, says, "If you invested $30,000 in a composite of the Dow Jones thirty years ago, it would be worth $134,000 today. If you had put that $30,000 into these [socially and ethically responsible] firms—$2,000 into each of the fifteen [in the study]—it would now be worth over $1 million." — John C. Maxwell, *There's No Such Thing as "Business" Ethics: There's Only One Rule for Making Decisions* (New York City, NY: FaithWords, 2007).

6. How common is lying and cheating? How common is a lack of integrity?

ON NOVEMBER 8, 2001, PEOPLE WERE SHOCKED WHEN one of the hottest companies of the booming nineties, Enron, admitted to using accounting practices that had inflated its income figures by $586 million over a four-year period.1 Less than a month later, Enron filed Chapter 11 bankruptcy, and early in 2002, the Justice Department launched a criminal investigation into the company's practices. Investigators wanted to determine how much executives knew about the company's status, as they told their employees to hold their shares of Enron stock, but sold more than $1 billion of their own.2 The company went belly-up, employees' retirement savings were all but wiped out, and millions of investors lost a total of more than $60 billion.3 Investors were stunned. And then the questions came: How could something like this happen? Why did it happen? Who let it happen?

A few months later, on March 27, 2002, the circle of people talking about ethics began to widen when the nation's sixth largest cable company, Adelphia Communications, announced that it also had financial problems. Founder John Rigas, along with his sons Timothy, Michael, and James, was accused of using company assets as collateral for loans totaling $3.1 billion to make personal purchases and finance family projects.4 After removing the Rigases, the company restated its earnings and later filed Chapter 11 bankruptcy. The value of its stock plummeted. On June 3, 2002, Adelphia was delisted from NASDAQ.5 Even more people became worried about ethics in business. And more people were asking questions: What kind of people would do such things? How could this happen? Could it happen again?

That very same day, Dennis Kozlowski, CEO of Tyco, was charged by the district attorney of Manhattan in New York City with evading $1 million in sales tax on artwork and other items he had purchased for himself with company funds.6 As investigators looked further into Kozlowski's actions, they alleged that he and two other Tyco executives had looted $600 million from the company.7 The worry about private unethical practices in business was becoming a very public concern.

Later that month, Time magazine declared it to be the "Summer of Mistrust" and reported, "Most Americans— 72% in the Time/CNN poll—fear that they see not a few isolated cases but a pattern of deception by a large number of companies."8 And that was before word got out about WorldCom, who announced that an internal audit found improper accounting procedures. Their profits from 2000 to 2002 had been overstated by $7.1 billion!9 And WorldCom said $3.8 billion in expenses had been improperly reported during five quarters. The consequences: Seventeen thousand workers lost their jobs, WorldCom restated its financial results (wiping out all profits during those quarters), and shares of its stock fell in value by 75 percent.10 And the questions in the mind of the public only increased: Why is this happening? How many companies are unethical? Whatever happened to business ethics? — John C. Maxwell, *There's No Such Thing as "Business" Ethics: There's Only One Rule for Making Decisions* (New York City, NY: FaithWords, 2007).

7. **So, integrity is good. Honesty is good. Let's all go out and try really hard to be honest. Let's all try**

really hard to be people of integrity. Is that the Christian message, or is there more to it than that?

This is how many people try to live the Christian life. They hear a sermon on gratefulness. They try really hard to be grateful. They do this for a few hours or a few days. Then, they forget about it. Life gets in the way. Then, they are left with a nagging feeling of guilt about how they are not as grateful as they would like to be.

Next week they hear a sermon on service. They try really hard to serve… for a few hours. Then they forget about it. Again, they have a life. They don't rebel against God or the idea of serving, they just forget about it and go on with life. But again, they are left with a nagging sense of guilt about not serving as they ought.

The next week they hear a sermon on prayer. Same thing.

There is a better way. (I owe my insight into this verse to John Ortberg. I think he got it from Dallas Willard.) Here is the key verse:

Train yourself to be godly. 1 Timothy 4:7 (NIV2011)

Let's go back to the piano. Instead of trying really hard to play Amazing Grace, what if you trained yourself to play Amazing Grace? What would that look like?

Let's imagine you sit down with a skilled piano teacher. He explains that your fingers can be numbered one through five. The thumb is one and the pinky is five. The middle finger is three.

He places your middle finger on the E above middle C. He asks you to play 3-2-1 starting with E above middle C with the middle finger of your right hand. These are the first three notes of "Mary had a little lamb." He walks you through the rest of the song, pointing to the notes on the music in front of you. After about ten times, you stumble through it.

He gives you ten more songs, and works you through each one until you are able to figure out how it works. He asks you to practice for an hour a day and you agree to do so. A week later, you can play the melody of all ten songs reasonably well. You are only playing one note at a time at this point.

He gives you ten more songs. You practice those for a few weeks. He introduces the left hand. At first, you play only the left hand. Then, you play both hands together. Then you play two notes at the same time in the right hand. This is called harmony. You practice some more. Practice, practice, practice. This is training to play the piano.

Keep this up for about five years and you will easily be able to play Amazing Grace. It won't be hard; it will be easy.

You might object that this way sounds like a hard way to learn to play Amazing Grace. It is not the hard way, it is the only way. The hard way is trying really hard to play Amazing Grace. Here is the good news. Once you subject yourself to this training, playing Amazing Grace will be easy. In fact, nearly any song in the hymnbook will be easy. Ask anyone who can play Amazing Grace. They will tell you it is easy. What is hard is trying to do something you have not trained yourself to do.

Train yourself to be godly. — Josh Hunt, *How to Live the Christian Life*, 2016.

8. **Why doesn't trying really hard work?**

   Some people would have us think that we must try really hard, live a certain way or do or not do certain things, and then we can be classified as "holy." However, to try to attain holiness is an impossible task. Instead, the Bible tells us that we become holy in God's eyes because of what Christ has done. "Those sanctified in Christ Jesus and called to be his holy people" (1 Corinthians 1:2). "For he chose us in him before the creation of the world to be holy and blameless in his sight" (Ephesians 1:4). "He has reconciled you by Christ's physical body through death to present you holy in his sight, without blemish and free from accusation" (Colossians 1:22). "God chose you as firstfruits to be saved through the sanctifying work of the Spirit and through belief in the truth" (2 Thessalonians 2:13).

   We mustn't get caught up in thinking that we must work hard to be holy. God has made us holy through Christ. — Livingstone Corporation, Len Woods, and Linda Taylor, *NIV, Once-a-Day: Bible Promises Devotional, Ebook* (Grand Rapids, MI: Zondervan, 2012).

9. **What does work?**

   Try as hard as you can, knowing that without Christ you can do nothing. Try as hard as you can knowing that you can do all this through Christ who strengthens you.

10. **Chapter 11: Fill Each Square with What Matters Most. What does Ortberg mean by that? How would you summarize the message of this chapter?**

    One morning, a wise professor stepped into his classroom determined to prove a point to a bunch of sleepy students. Under his arm he carried a big, widemouthed jar. He made his way to the front of the room and placed the jar on his desk. With the students paying little attention, he filled the jar with five big stones. He put the stones in one by one until the jar couldn't hold anymore. Then he asked his students, "Is this jar full?" They half-nodded their assertion that it was.

The professor pulled a bucket of pebbles from under his desk. Slowly, he poured the pebbles into the jar. They bounced and settled into the small spaces that had been created between the stones. Once again, the professor asked his students, who were now slightly more awake, "Is this jar full?" They all quietly contended that, yes, of course it was.

The professor proceeded to pull another bucket from beneath his desk, this one filled with fine sand. As the students looked on, he poured the bucket of sand into the jar. The granules quickly filled in the barely visible cracks and crevices left between the stones and pebbles. This time when asked, "Is this jar full?" the class answered with a resounding, "Yes!"

In response to his students' certainty, the professor reached under his desk and brought out a pitcher of water. The students watched in amazement as the professor poured the entire pitcher of water into the jar.

Then the professor asked a different question. "What was the point of this illustration?"

A student in the back called out, "You were showing us that you can always fit more into your life if you really work at it."

"No, that's not it," the professor answered. "The point is that you have to put the big rocks in first, or you'll never get them in. These five rocks are your top priorities. Carefully consider what they are, get them set, and everything else will fall into place around them." — Nelson Searcy and Jennifer Dykes Henson, *The Generosity Ladder: Your Next Step to Financial Peace* (Grand Rapids, MI: Baker Books, 2010), 95–97.

11. Another Google Bible Study. What does the Bible have to say about putting the big rocks in first?

Answer: Time management is important because of the brevity of our lives. Our earthly sojourn is significantly shorter than we are inclined to think. As David so aptly points out, "You have made my days a mere handbreadth; the span of my years is as nothing before you. Each man's life is but a breath" (Psalm 39:4–5). The apostle James echoes this: "You are a mist that appears for a little while and then vanishes" (James 4:14). Indeed, our time on earth is fleeting—in fact, it is infinitesimally small compared to eternity. To live as God would have us live, it is essential we make the best possible use of our allotted time.

Moses prays, "Teach us to number our days, that we may gain a heart of wisdom" (Psalm 90:12). A good way to gain wisdom is to learn to live each day with an eternal perspective. Our Creator has set eternity in our hearts (Ecclesiastes 3:11). Knowing that we will have to give an account to the One who gives us time should motivate us to use it well. C. S. Lewis understood this: "If you read history you will find that the Christians who did the most for the present world were just those who thought most of the next."

In his letter to the Ephesians, Paul cautioned the saints, "Be very careful, then, how you live—not as unwise but as wise, making the most of every opportunity, because the days are evil" (Ephesians 5:15–16). Living wisely involves using our time carefully. Knowing that the harvest is great and the workers are few (Luke 10:2) and that time is rapidly dwindling should help us make better use of our time to witness, both through our words and our example. We are to spend time loving others in deed and in truth (1 John 3:17–18). https://www.gotquestions.org/Bible-time-management.html

12. Matthew 6.33. First things first. What is the first priority of every Christian?

Life is a lot like a coin; you can spend it any way you wish, but you can spend it only once. Choosing one thing over all the rest throughout life is a difficult thing to do. This is especially true when the choices are so many and the possibilities are so close at hand.

To be completely truthful with you, however, we aren't left with numerous possibilities. Jesus Himself gave us the top priority: "Seek first His kingdom and His righteousness." . . .

If I am to seek first in my life God's kingdom and God's righteousness, then whatever else I do ought to relate to that goal: where I work, with whom I spend my time, the one I marry, or the decision to remain single. Every decision I make ought to be filtered through the Matthew 6:33 filter. — Living Above the Level of Mediocrity / Charles R. Swindoll, *Wisdom for the Way: Wise Words for Busy People* (Nashville: Thomas Nelson, 2007).

13. What exactly is meant by the "kingdom of God"?

Where is the kingdom of God? Comprehensive theological studies have debated the complexities of this question for centuries, but let me suggest a simplified answer from Scripture: The kingdom of God is wherever Jesus is king! If Jesus is king in your heart, then the kingdom of God is within you (see Luke 17:21). Because Jesus is king in heaven, then the kingdom of God is also in heaven (see Psalm 103:19). While Jesus walked the earth, He used miracles to announce that the kingdom of God was with them (see Luke 11:20), and when the reign of Christ is fully realized on earth, then the kingdom of God is on earth (see Revelation 5:10).

What is the kingdom of God? It is the rule and reign of God! When we pray "Thy kingdom come, thy will be done," we are praying a redundant statement. Whenever God's will is done, the kingdom has come. The two phrases say the same thing. The reason we pray "Thy kingdom come, Thy will be done in earth, as it is in heaven" (Matthew 6:10, KJV) is because God's will is done perfectly in heaven but imperfectly on earth. — Rick Warren, "Foreword," in *The Kingdom Life: A Practical Theology of Discipleship and Spiritual Formation,* ed. Alan Andrews (Colorado Springs, CO: NavPress, 2010), 7–8.

14. What good things come to those who seek first the kingdom?

Seek first the kingdom of wealth, and you'll worry over every dollar. Seek first the kingdom of health, and you'll sweat every blemish and bump. Seek first the kingdom of popularity, and you'll relive every conflict. Seek first the kingdom of safety, and you'll jump at every crack of the twig. But seek first his kingdom, and you will find it. On that, we can depend and never worry. — Max Lucado, *Fearless: Imagine Your Life without Fear* (Nashville: Thomas Nelson, 2012).

15. 1 Timothy 5.8. What does this verse teach about priorities?

The basic priority of values is as follows: (1) God comes before persons (Matt. 10:37); (2) one's family comes before others (I Tim. 5:8); (3) persons come before things (Mark 8:36). Not all Christians agree on the details of these priorities, but all must seek the Scriptures to discover in every situation what is the "greatest commandment" and which is the "least." — Norman L. Geisler, Paul D. Feinberg, and Paul D. Feinberg, *Introduction to Philosophy: A Christian Perspective* (Grand Rapids, MI: Baker Book House, 1980), 427.

Our first priority, of course, is our family, if we have one (1 Tim. 5:8). — Max E. Anders and Max E. Anders, *30 Days to Understanding the Christian Life in 15 Minutes a Day* (Nashville: T. Nelson, 1998), 124.

16. Everyone knows family ought to be the priority. But, many people don't actually live that way. Why is this?

Dr. Robert Schuller was on a whirlwind book promotion tour, visiting eight cities in four days. It was exhausting work in addition to his normal duties as pastor of a large church.

As Schuller reviewed his schedule with his secretary, she reminded him that he was scheduled to have lunch with the winner of a charity raffle. Schuller was suddenly sobered when he found out the winner of the raffle, for he happened to know that the $500 the person had bid to have lunch with him represented that person's entire life savings.

The winner was his own teenage daughter. —Steve Farrar, *Standing Tall* (Multnomah, 1994) / Craig Brian

Larson and Phyllis Ten Elshof, *1001 Illustrations That Connect* (Grand Rapids, MI: Zondervan Publishing House, 2008), 292.

17. The last priority is calling. Are callings for preachers, or for all of us?

Hang around preachers enough, and you're sure to hear the word calling come up. Most every preacher you meet has his own story of how God called him into the ministry. I wonder, however, if other believers ever think about God calling them to, well...anything at all.

While I know for certain that my call from God to full-time ministry was real and tangible, I am fully convinced that God doesn't just reserve the calling to the prophetic fraternity. Why? Because Moses was an average guy, David was a shepherd, and Amos was a fig farmer.

The scriptures say that you are "fearfully and wonderfully made" (Psalm 139:14). God took time to make you, and He doesn't waste His energy creating a worthless product.

Every one of us is called to something. Calling is not a guarantee of success or of failure. Calling is not exclusive to any group, like, say, pastors. Your calling is, however, unique to you. Most importantly, calling is about obedience, not the task ahead.

Following your calling comes down to courage and guts. Do you have the fortitude to stay on a path when it gets hard or to go where God tells you to go even though life is comfortable?

My calling has been, and always will be, the only constant I can truly depend on in terms of my career and my identity. My identity is shaped by the fact that

God told me He wanted me walking a certain path. You have the same kind of calling. The context of your career may not be the same as mine, but your decision to be obedient to His call on your life is what's at stake.

Never be afraid to walk into the unknown when God has called you to do it. It's there and only there that you'll find a freedom that transcends circumstance. — Jason Cruise, *The Man Minute: A 60-Second Encounter Can Change Your Life* (Uhrichsville, OH: Barbour, 2015).

18. How do I discover my calling?

It's very important for you to find what God had in mind when he first thought you up. A calling is something you discover, not something you choose, so I want to give you some questions to help you find your calling:

1. What's My Raw Material?

God has given you DNA, certain predispositions, a temperament, and talents, and you have to honor this raw material that you've been given. So you need to ask yourself questions like, "What sorts of things do other people tell me I do well?" or, "What have I done well in the past?" Write down your important life achievements. What were some things in the early days of your life that you were good at?

2. What Work Brings Me Joy?

What do you have a desire for—a passion? It's not an accident that your spirit rejoices in certain activities. That, too, is part of what God has placed in you. What do you love to do? What is it that brings you to life?

3. What Are My Expectations?

There's a big difference between loving to do certain activities or tasks for their own sake because you were made to love them, and wanting a job because you think you want the rewards or status or prestige that might flow out of it. There's a big difference between doing a task because God calls you to it, and just doing what your father, or friends, or your ego wants you to do.

4. What Are My Limitations?

What's the one limitation in your life that is the most painful for you to accept? If you can acknowledge and embrace all of your limitedness, you will have made tremendous strides down the road to understanding your calling.

According to the Bible, you have a calling, and it has to do with what God hardwired into you. You must seek it with an open, submitted spirit. When people try to pretend that they're something they're not, they live with a chronic sense of inadequacy. They set themselves up for a lifetime of frustrations. Don't do that. Be ruthlessly open to the truth about yourself. Your calling is something you discover, not something you choose.
— John Ortberg, *Now What? God's Guide to Life for Graduates* (Grand Rapids, MI: Zondervan, 2011).

19. What do you want to remember from today's study?

20. How can we pray for each other this week?

When the Game is Over, Lesson #6
Chapters 12 - 14
Roll the Dice
Play with Gratitude
Find Your Mission
Good Questions Have Groups Talking
www.joshhunt.com

OPEN:

Would is one thing you are grateful for today?

DIG

1. **Chapter 12. How would you summarize the message of this chapter? Feel free to peek.**

   Here is the irrefutable truth about games that my grandmother would try to teach me as she risked everything for Boardwalk while I tried to hang on to my little cache: when you start the game, you never know what the outcome will be. If you play the game, you may lose. But if you never play the game, you definitely will never win.

   And if you play the game, you have to roll the dice. — John Ortberg, *When the Game Is Over, It All Goes Back in the Box* (Grand Rapids, MI: Zondervan, 2008).

2. **Ecclesiastes 11.4 is communicated as a word-picture. How would you communicate this in straightforward, non-metaphorical language?**

The language in which this proverb is couched is taken from the harvest field and is therefore peculiarly applicable at this season.3 That does not mean, of course, that the way to succeed in farming is entirely to disregard the weather. But it means that if farmers will not work except when all the conditions for their work are perfect, if they are always doubting and fearing and forecasting rain, worrying and fretting instead of making the best of things, then probably they will neither sow nor reap and are little likely to make successful farmers. Just as a person may fail through too much zeal, so may a person fail through too much prudence. — Diana Wallis, *Take Heart: Daily Devotions with the Church's Great Preachers* (Grand Rapids, MI: Kregel Publications, 2001), 292.

3. **Read for application; always read for application. What is the application of this verse?**

I clearly remember driving down a familiar road in my car. As trees whizzed by my thoughts were a blur too. I mentally ran through my list of good intentions that always followed this phrase, "When things are normal then I'll . . ." (fill in the blank with "exercise," "eat better," "have a longer quiet time"). Suddenly I mentally slammed on the brakes as I realized I had been having the same conversation with myself on this same road for five years.

I whispered to myself, "Normal isn't coming."

That actually became the beginning of the "Do What You Can" Plan because I resolved in that moment to begin making small changes now rather than waiting for the perfect time later. Guess what? The perfect time doesn't exist. There will always be a complication, a crisis, or what looks like a legitimate reason to wait.

Start now or you may not ever start. — Holley Gerth, *The "Do What You Can" Plan (ebook Shorts): 21 Days to Making Any Area of Your Life Better* (Grand Rapids, MI: Revell, 2013).

4. **Mark 6.45ff. What do we learn about rolling the dice from this story?**

You can live on bland food so as to avoid an ulcer, drink no tea, coffee or other stimulants in the name of health, go to bed early, stay away from night life, avoid all controversial subjects so as never to give offense, mind your own business, avoid involvement in other people's problems, spend money only on necessities and save all you can.

You can still break your neck in the bath tub, and it will serve you right.

Larry Laudan, a philosopher of science, has spent the last decade studying risk-management. He writes of how we live in a society so fear-driven that we suffer from what he calls risk-lock—a condition which, like gridlock, leaves us unable to do anything or go anywhere. He summarizes literature on risk management in nineteen principles. The first principle is the simplest: Everything is risky. If you're looking for absolute safety, you chose the wrong species. You can stay home in bed—but that may make you one of the half-million Americans who require emergency room treatment each year for injuries sustained while falling out of bed. You can cover your windows—but that may make you one of the ten people a year who accidentally hang themselves on the cords of their venetian blinds. You can hide your money in a mattress—but that may make you one of tens of thousands of the people who go to the emergency room each year because of wounds caused by handling money—everything from paper cuts to (for the wealthy) hernias.

If you step up to the plate, you may strike out. The greatest hitters in the world fail two times out of three.

But it you don't step up to the plate, you will never know the glory of what it is to hit a home run. There is danger in getting out of the boat. But there is danger in staying in it as well. If you live in the boat—whatever your boat happens to be—you will eventually die of boredom and stagnation. Everything is risky. — John Ortberg, *If You Want to Walk on Water, You've Got to Get out of the Boat* (Grand Rapids, MI: Zondervan, 2008).

5. What risk did Peter take in this story?

Now we come to a part of the story you may not like very much. I don't care for it much myself. The choice to follow Jesus—the choice to grow—is the choice for the constant recurrence of fear. You've got to get out of the boat a little every day.

Let me explain. The disciples get into the boat, face the storm, see the water-walker, and are afraid. "Don't be afraid," Jesus says. Peter then girds up his loins, asks permission to go overboard, sees the wind, and is afraid all over again. "Don't be afraid," Jesus says. Do you think that's the last time in his life Peter will experience fear?

Here is a deep truth about water-walking: The fear will never go away. Why? Because each time I want to grow, it will involve going into new territory, taking on new challenges. And each time I do that, I will experience fear again. As Susan Jeffers writes, "The fear will never go away, as long as I continue to grow."

Never! Isn't that great news? Now you can give up trying to make fear go away. Fear and growth go together like macaroni and cheese. It's a package deal. The decision to grow always involves a choice between risk and comfort. This means that to be a follower of Jesus you must renounce comfort as the ultimate value of your life. And that's sobering news to most of us, because we're into comfort. Theologian Karl Barth said that comfort is one of the great siren calls of our age.

Would you like to guess the name of the best-selling chair in America?

La-Z-Boy.

Not Risk-E-Boy.

Not Work-R-Boy.

La-Z-Boy. We want to immerse ourselves in comfort. We have developed a whole language around this. People say, "I want to go home and veg out—make myself as much like vegetation as humanly possible, preferably in front of a television set." — John Ortberg, *If You Want to Walk on Water, You've Got to Get out of the Boat* (Grand Rapids, MI: Zondervan, 2008).

6. What bad things happen to those who don't get out of the boat?

We have a name for people who do this in front of TV, too: couch potatoes. Couch potatoes in their La-Z-Boys.

The eleven disciples could be called "boat potatoes." They didn't mind watching, but they didn't want to actually do anything.

Millions of people in churches these days could be called "pew potatoes." They want some of the comfort associated with spirituality, but they don't want the risk and challenge that go along with actually following Jesus. Yet Jesus is still looking for people who will get out of the boat. He is looking for someone who will say, if you'll pardon the expression, "I may be small potatoes, Lord, but this spud's for you."

And as we will see in this book, both choices—risk and comfort—tend to grow into a habit. Each time you get out of the boat, you become a little more likely to get out the next time. It's not that the fear goes away, but that you get used to living with fear. You realize that it does not have the power to destroy you.

On the other hand, every time you resist that voice, every time you choose to stay in the boat rather than heed its call, the voice gets a little quieter in you. Then at last you don't hear its call at all. — John Ortberg, *If You Want to Walk on Water, You've Got to Get out of the Boat* (Grand Rapids, MI: Zondervan, 2008).

7. Peter took his eyes off Jesus and sank. Did he fail?

As a result of seeing the wind and giving in to fear, Peter began to sink into the water. So here is the question: Did Peter fail? Before I offer an answer, let me make an observation about failure, because in this book we talk a lot about it.

Failure is not an event, but rather a judgment about an event. Failure is not something that happens to us or a label we attach to things. It is a way we think about outcomes.

Before Jonas Salk developed a vaccine for polio that finally worked, he tried two hundred unsuccessful ones. Somebody asked him, "How did it feel to fail two hundred times?"

"I never failed two hundred times in my life," Salk replied. "I was taught not to use the word 'failure.' I just discovered two hundred ways how not to vaccinate for polio."

Somebody once asked Winston Churchill what most prepared him to risk political suicide by speaking out against Hitler during the years of appeasement in the mid–1930s, then to lead Great Britain against Nazi Germany. Churchill said it was the time he had to repeat a grade in elementary school.

"You mean you failed a year in grade school?" he was asked.

"I never failed anything in my life. I was given a second opportunity to get it right."

Jonas Salk made two hundred unsuccessful attempts to create a polio vaccine. Was Jonas Salk a failure?

Winston Churchill repeated a grade in elementary school. Was Winston Churchill a failure?

I grew up in northern Illinois and have rooted for the Chicago Cubs my entire life. As of this writing, the Cubs have not been in the World Series for fifty-four years. In fact, they have not won the World Series for ninety years. Are the Chicago Cubs a failure?

Okay, bad example.

Did Peter fail?

Well, I suppose in a way he did. His faith wasn't strong enough. His doubts were stronger. "He saw the wind."

He took his eyes off of where they should have been. He sank. He failed.

But here is what I think. I think there were eleven bigger failures sitting in the boat. They failed quietly. They failed privately. Their failure went unnoticed, unobserved, uncriticized. Only Peter knew the shame of public failure. — John Ortberg, *If You Want to Walk on Water, You've Got to Get out of the Boat* (Grand Rapids, MI: Zondervan, 2008).

8. **Chapter 13. Play with gratitude. What Bible verses can you find on the importance of gratitude?**

    Psalm 7:17 I will give thanks to the LORD because of his righteousness; I will sing the praises of the name of the LORD Most High.

    Psalm 9:1 I will give thanks to you, LORD, with all my heart; I will tell of all your wonderful deeds.

    Psalm 28:7 The LORD is my strength and my shield; my heart trusts in him, and he helps me. My heart leaps for joy, and with my song I praise him.

    Psalm 35:18 I will give you thanks in the great assembly; among the throngs I will praise you.

    Psalm 52:9 For what you have done I will always praise you in the presence of your faithful people. And I will hope in your name, for your name is good.

    Psalm 54:6 I will sacrifice a freewill offering to you; I will praise your name, LORD, for it is good.

    Psalm 69:30 I will praise God's name in song and glorify him with thanksgiving.

Psalm 79:13 Then we your people, the sheep of your pasture, will praise you forever; from generation to generation we will proclaim your praise.

9. What benefits come to the grateful?

Two psychologists, Dr. Robert A. Emmons of the University of California, Davis, and Dr. Michael E. McCullough of the University of Miami, have done much of the research on gratitude. In one study, they asked all participants to write a few sentences each week, focusing on particular topics.

One group wrote about things they were grateful for that had occurred during the week. A second group wrote about daily irritations or things that had displeased them, and the third wrote about events that had affected them (with no emphasis on them being positive or negative). After 10 weeks, those who wrote about gratitude were more optimistic and felt better about their lives. Surprisingly, they also exercised more and had fewer visits to physicians than those who focused on sources of aggravation.

Another leading researcher in this field, Dr. Martin E. P. Seligman, a psychologist at the University of Pennsylvania, tested the impact of various positive psychology interventions on 411 people, each compared with a control assignment of writing about early memories. When their week's assignment was to write and personally deliver a letter of gratitude to someone who had never been properly thanked for his or her kindness, participants immediately exhibited a huge increase in happiness scores. This impact was greater than that from any other intervention, with benefits lasting for a month.

10. How can we be grateful when life is hard?

The feeling of gratitude comes easily when good things happen. But that gratitude is fleeting. When good things come to you easily and quickly without much effort, the feeling of gratitude is even more short-lived.

The discipline of gratitude is a different matter. To have wished for, put every ounce of effort to, pinned your hopes and dreams on, and then bet the farm on that one thing—and then to receive it—that gratitude runs deep and long.

There's a greater, deeper gratitude still. It's gratitude chiseled from what we did not ask for, gratitude for something we had not perceived as a wished-for life requirement. This gratitude comes when we look about us at all we do not have. We know very well what we did not get, even though we longed for it. In fact the landscape at that moment is like the charcoal scape of Death Valley, or the wilderness in Israel, or the Sahara desert. We don't see a thing to be grateful for. That is when practicing the discipline of gratitude is most precious, rewarding, and transforming.

One writer challenged his readers to list one thousand things they were thankful for. Don't start with that large a goal. But start somewhere.

By looking for that one tiny thing to be thankful for, you are sending a signal to your entire being that you are not bound by the present and that the best is yet to come. I introduced two young widows to each other. We were practicing gratitude that day. One husband had died due to a three-year battle with cancer. The other had been lost in a tragic, sudden accident. Both women were single-parenting young children, not an easy task. One was grateful they had time to say goodbye; the other was grateful that there was no long period of suffering and pain. They were each making a choice in their circumstances, choosing gratitude. — Miriam Neff, *Where Do I Go from Here? Bold Living after Unwanted Change* (Chicago, IL: Moody Publishers, 2012).

11. Is gratitude an emotion or a decision?

Gratitude is such a great and wonderful thing in Scripture that I feel constrained to end this chapter with a tribute. There are ways that gratitude helps bring about obedience to Christ. One way is that the spirit of gratitude is simply incompatible with some sinful attitudes. I think this is why Paul wrote, "There must be no filthiness and silly talk, or coarse jesting, which are not fitting, but rather giving of thanks" (Ephesians 5:4). Gratitude is a humble, happy response to the good will of someone who has done or tried to do you a favor. This humility and happiness cannot coexist in the heart with coarse, ugly, mean attitudes. Therefore the cultivation of a thankful heart leaves little room for such sins. — John Piper, *Future Grace* (Sisters, OR: Multnomah Publishers, 1995), 48.

12. I had to think about this one for a bit: how are gratitude and faith related?

There is a sense in which gratitude and faith are interwoven joys that strengthen each other. As gratitude joyfully revels in the benefits of past grace, so faith joyfully relies on the benefits of future grace. Therefore when gratitude for God's past grace is strong, the message is sent that God is supremely trustworthy in the future because of what he has done in the past. In this way faith is strengthened by a lively gratitude for God's past trustworthiness.

On the other hand, when faith in God's future grace is strong, the message is sent that this kind of God makes no mistakes, so that everything he has done in the past is part of a good plan and can be remembered with gratitude. In this way gratitude is strengthened by a lively faith in God's future grace. Surely it is only the heart of faith in future grace that can follow the apostle Paul in "giving thanks for all things in the name of our Lord Jesus Christ" (Ephesians 5:20). Only if we trust God to turn past calamities into future comfort can we look back with gratitude for all things.

It seems to me that this interwovenness of future-oriented faith and past-oriented gratitude is what prevents gratitude from degenerating into the debtor's ethic. Gratitude for bygone grace is constantly saying to faith, "Be strong, and do not doubt that God will be as gracious in the future as I know he's been in the past." And faith in future grace is constantly saying to gratitude, "There is more grace to come, and all our obedience is to be done in reliance on that future grace. Relax and exult in your appointed feast. I will take responsibility for tomorrow's obedience."

Or, as Jesus would say, "O ye of little faith. Do not be anxious" (Matthew 6:30–31, KJV). — John Piper, *Future Grace* (Sisters, OR: Multnomah Publishers, 1995), 48–49.

13. **Chapter 14. Find your mission. How many would say it is true of you—that you have found your mission? How did you find your mission?**

Da Vinci painted one Mona Lisa. Beethoven composed one Fifth Symphony. And God made one version of you. He custom designed you for a one-of-a-kind assignment.

Mine like a gold digger the unique-to-you nuggets from your life.

When I was six years old, my father built us a house. Architectural Digest didn't notice, but my mom sure did. Dad constructed it, board by board, every day after work. My youth didn't deter him from giving me a job. He tied an empty nail apron around my waist, placed a magnet in my hands, and sent me on daily patrols around the building site, carrying my magnet only inches off the ground.

One look at my tools and you could guess my job. Stray-nail collector.

One look at yours and the same can be said. Brick by brick, life by life, God is creating a kingdom, a "spiritual house" (1 Pet. 2:5 CEV). He entrusted you with a key task in the project. Examine your tools and discover it. Your ability unveils your destiny. "If anyone ministers, let him do it as with the ability which God supplies, that in all things God may be glorified through Jesus Christ" (1 Pet. 4:11). When God gives an assignment, he also gives the skill. Study your skills, then, to reveal your assignment.

Look at you. Your uncanny ease with numbers. Your quenchless curiosity about chemistry. Others stare at blueprints and yawn; you read them and drool. "I was made to do this," you say.

Heed that inner music. No one else hears it the way you do. — Max Lucado, *Cure for the Common Life: Living in Your Sweet Spot* (Nashville, TN: Thomas Nelson Publishers, 2005), 2.

14. What benefits come to those who find their mission?

And enough of its arrogant opposite: "I have to do everything." No, you don't! You're not God's solution to society, but a solution in society. Imitate Paul, who said, "Our goal is to stay within the boundaries of God's plan for us" (2 Cor. 10:13 NLT). Clarify your contribution.

Don't worry about skills you don't have. Don't covet strengths others do have. Just extract your uniqueness. "Kindle afresh the gift of God which is in you" (2 Tim. 1:6 NASB). And do so to ...make a big deal out of God. — Max Lucado, Cure for the Common Life: Living in Your Sweet Spot (Nashville, TN: Thomas Nelson Publishers, 2005), 4.

15. Preachers sometimes speak of calling. Does everyone have a calling, or just preachers?

Hang around preachers enough, and you're sure to hear the word calling come up. Most every preacher you meet has his own story of how God called him into the ministry. I wonder, however, if other believers ever think about God calling them to, well...anything at all.

While I know for certain that my call from God to full-time ministry was real and tangible, I am fully convinced that God doesn't just reserve the calling to the prophetic fraternity. Why? Because Moses was an average guy, David was a shepherd, and Amos was a fig farmer.

The scriptures say that you are "fearfully and wonderfully made" (Psalm 139:14). God took time to make you, and He doesn't waste His energy creating a worthless product.

Every one of us is called to something. Calling is not a guarantee of success or of failure. Calling is not exclusive to any group, like, say, pastors. Your calling is, however, unique to you. Most importantly, calling is about obedience, not the task ahead. — Jason Cruise, *The Man Minute: A 60-Second Encounter Can Change Your Life* (Uhrichsville, OH: Barbour, 2015).

16. 2 Thessalonians 1.11. What does "calling" mean in this context?

Outside of the New Testament, calling usually signifies vocation, position, or station in life. One's calling is law or medicine, education or business, family or perhaps the family business. But the idea of calling has even greater significance for Christians.

If you're a believer, your salvation is an act of God. By His mercy and grace, He called you out of darkness into an eternal love relationship that is completely undeserved.

But God's calling to His people is much more than a vocation; it is a divine invitation to participate in His will and the work of His kingdom. We should consider our calling the highest privilege life offers; it means we are chosen by God.

God initiates our calling and reveals it to us through His Holy Spirit. His Spirit then guides and empowers as we serve God not only in our vocation but also by participating in His kingdom work.

God has a purpose for your life, and it involves far more than earning a living. — Henry Blackaby and Richard Blackaby, *Being Still with God Every Day* (Nashville: Thomas Nelson, 2014).

17. Is your calling something you choose, or is it chosen for you?

Every human being on this earth has a calling. There are no un-called human beings. You have a purpose. You have a design. It was conceived by God, and it is essential to God's dream for the human community.

A calling is not primarily about increasing your earning potential or status or prestige. A calling refers to the fact that God made you with certain capacities, and this world needs you to use those abilities.

To fulfill your calling is a noble thing. It's at the core of human existence. If you watch people who are fulfilling their callings, their motivation level is high; when obstacles come along, they have amazing endurance to overcome them. They're growing and learning, and there's joy in what they do. To miss out on your calling is to miss out on a large part of the reason why you walk this planet, and why you were made by God.

Some people think that only certain categories of folks have a calling—pastors, maybe, or Billy Graham, or Mother Teresa. That's not true. The Bible is very, very clear that whether your job is in a church or in the world of business, wherever it is, every human being is created by God, gifted by God, and called by God. You have a calling, and you had better take your calling seriously.

It's very important for you to find what God had in mind when he first thought you up. A calling is something you discover, not something you choose. — John Ortberg, *Now What? God's Guide to Life for Graduates* (Grand Rapids, MI: Zondervan, 2011).

18. I want to find my mission. What advice do you have for me?

At this very moment in another section of the church building in which I write, little kids explore their tools. Preschool classrooms may sound like a cacophony to you and me, but God hears a symphony.

A five-year-old sits at a crayon-strewn table. He seldom talks. Classmates have long since set aside their papers, but he ponders his. The colors compel him. He marvels at the gallery of kelly green and navy blue and royal purple. Masterpiece in hand, he'll race to Mom and Dad, eager to show them his kindergarten Picasso.

His sister, however, forgets her drawing. She won't consume the home commute with tales of painted pictures. She'll tell tales of tales. "The teacher told us a new story today!" And the girl will need no prodding to repeat it.

Another boy cares less about the story and the drawings and more about the other kids. He spends the day wearing a "Hey, listen to me!" expression, lingering at the front of the class, testing the patience of the teacher. He relishes attention, evokes reactions. His theme seems to be "Do it this way. Come with me. Let's try this."

Meaningless activities at an insignificant age? Or subtle hints of hidden strengths? I opt for the latter. The quiet boy with the color fascination may someday brighten city walls with murals. His sister may pen a screenplay or teach literature to curious coeds. And the kid who recruits followers today might eventually do the same on behalf of a product, the poor, or even his church.

What about you? Our Maker gives assignments to people, "to each according to each one's unique ability"

(Matt. 25:15).1 As he calls, he equips. Look back over your life. What have you consistently done well? What have you loved to do? Stand at the intersection of your affections and successes and find your uniqueness.

You have one. A divine spark.2 An uncommon call to an uncommon life. "The Spirit has given each of us a special way of serving others" (1 Cor. 12:7 CEV). So much for the excuse "I don't have anything to offer." Did the apostle Paul say, "The Spirit has given some of us ..."? Or, "The Spirit has given a few of us ..."? No. "The Spirit has given each of us a special way of serving others." Enough of this self-deprecating "I can't do anything." — Max Lucado, *Cure for the Common Life: Living in Your Sweet Spot* (Nashville, TN: Thomas Nelson Publishers, 2005), 2–4.

19. What did you learn today? What do you want to remember and apply?

20. How an we pray for each other this week?

When the Game is Over, Lesson #7
Chapters 15, 16
Beware the Shadow Mission
Two Cheers for Competition
Good Questions Have Groups Talking
www.joshhunt.com

OPEN:

What sports did you play growing up? What sports do you watch today?

DIG

1. **Last week we talked about finding you calling. Did you do any thinking about that this week? Who has a calling, and why is it important that you find yours?**

    I was speaking in Saskatoon, a city I'd never heard of until the conference organizers called. It sounded like the name of Bugs Bunny's hometown, but I discovered it was a real city in Saskatchewan, Canada. It was a cold November day, but the smiling and nodding from a woman in the audience sitting about ten rows back toward the right side of the stage warmed my heart. I'll never forget her. She nodded, laughed, and even nudged her girlfriend next to her every time I made a great point. I spoke three times that day to a conference of 1,200 women and she shone like a bright light, giving me a boost of energy and confidence every time I looked her way. During my book signing at the end of the day, she came through the line.

"I remember you!" I said, happy to have a chance to meet and thank her. "You were sitting in about the tenth row, a little to my right."

Shocked that I had noticed her in the audience and actually remembered where she was sitting, she said, "Do you remember where everyone in the audience sat?"

"No, I sure don't. But I remember you. Every time I looked your way you were smiling and energetic. Let me ask you something. Is it your mission to bring joy to people?" I said.

She looked both perplexed and elated. "Can my mission really be that simple?" she asked. "People at work tell me I bring them joy all the time! I've been trying to figure out what my mission is. I didn't know it could be that simple!"

Your mission is not complicated. It is a simple, one-sentence description. And if you have not yet articulated it, know this: Your mission is to love and serve others using your gifts, strengths, and resources. So until you get clear about the specifics, embrace that as your mission and I guarantee you'll be on the right track. — Valorie Burton, *Your 5-Minute Personal Coach: Ask the Right Questions, Get the Right Answers* (Eugene, OR: Harvest House, 2012).

2. What keeps us from our calling?

The way we express our mission at my church is:

> Love God, Love People, Turn the World Upside Down

We're to have intimacy with God and people, and then have influence on the world according to the unique way God made us. But I could express my personal mission this way:

> Love God, Love People, Win Fantasy Football

If I'm honest, I generally prefer to pour myself into making sure my fake football team wins in my fake football league instead of having a real, eternal impact with my life. A guy I spend time with every week would probably say his personal mission is:

> Love God, Love People, Play Video Games

It's true. His every spare moment is devoted to playing Xbox. His biggest goals in life are defeating people he's never met who play against him online. I have a bunch of friends who could express their mission this way:

> Love God, Love People, Make Sure My Kids Grow Up to Become Successful

Sure, we could argue that if their kids end up successful, the parents maybe had some influence on the world through them. But that's not their motivation. They want their kids to have what they never had, or they are driven by fears about their kids' futures. They may have a need to prove themselves through their kids, or they've totally embraced the American Dream even though it doesn't match God's dreams. — Vince Antonucci, *Renegade: Your Faith Isn't Meant to Be Safe* (Grand Rapids, MI: Baker, 2013).

3. Chapter 15. What does Ortberg mean by a shadow mission?

One of my favorite authors writes about a men's retreat he attended where the guys sat in a circle and discussed their calling. They were each encouraged to talk about the mission God had for their lives, and they were challenged to think about how they might miss it and instead live out a "shadow mission."

> Just as we all have a mission—a way of contributing to God's kingdom that we were designed and gifted for—we also have what might be called a shadow mission. My shadow mission is what I will do with my life if I drift on autopilot. It consists of the activities toward which I will gravitate if I allow my natural temptations and selfishness to take over. Everybody has a shadow mission.

> By way of illustration, one of the staff members told us, "My shadow mission is to watch television and masturbate while the world goes to hell." A round of nervous laughter swept across the circle of men.

> "I'm going to say it one more time," the man said, "only this time I want you to listen and not laugh." And then he said it again: "My shadow mission is to watch television and . . ."

> This time the silence was sobering. Each of us was thinking the same thing: how easily any of our lives can slide into such a self-centered, trivial pursuit. He wasn't tempted to be Adolph Hitler or Saddam Hussein. The man would have fought against that kind of outright evil. It was the banality of his shadow mission that made it so possible.[46]

God has a calling for each of our lives, but there's a problem. God typically calls us to an uncomfortable mission. We prefer our calling to be comfortable, thank you very much.

And so we refuse to give ourselves to God's mission for our lives. But we will give ourselves to something. Something will become the object of our obsession. Something will be what we pour our time into. Something will be our attempt at greatness.

And our "somethings" tend to be things that are safe and selfish. — Vince Antonucci, *Renegade: Your Faith Isn't Meant to Be Safe* (Grand Rapids, MI: Baker, 2013).

4. Is the shadow mission like our calling, or no?

They are almost always slight variations of our authentic missions. This is part of what makes them seductive. Rarely is somebody's shadow mission 180 degrees in the wrong direction. Our shadow missions generally involve the gifts and passions that have been hardwired into us. It's just that we are tempted to misuse them ever so slightly. Our shadow mission leads us just five or ten degrees off our true path in the direction of selfishness or comfort or arrogance. But those few degrees, over time, become the difference between light and shadow. — John Ortberg, *Overcoming Your Shadow Mission* (Grand Rapids, MI: Zondervan, 2008).

5. What was Jesus' shadow mission?

Did Jesus face a shadow mission? I think so. We are told by the writer of Hebrews that he, like us, was tempted "in every way"—but was without sin (4:15). For Jesus, the shadow mission was to be a leader without suffering, the Messiah without the cross.

The great New Testament scholar F. F. Bruce writes, "Time and again the temptation came to him from many directions to choose some less costly way of fulfilling that calling than the way of suffering and death, but he resisted it to the end and set his face steadfastly to accomplish the purpose for which he had come into the world."*

You remember that in the desert Satan tempts Jesus to achieve his mission without hunger, "Turn these stones to bread. You don't need to be hungry" without pain, "Throw yourself down from the temple, and the angels will bear you up" without opposition, "Bow down before me, and all the kingdoms of the earth will be yours." You don't have to be hungry, you don't have to hurt, you don't have to be opposed.

Later on, when Jesus tells the disciples he must suffer and die, Peter tries to convince him that his suffering is unnecessary. This is the same shadow mission, and that is why Jesus rebukes Peter so sharply, saying, "Get behind me, Satan!"

Jesus' shadow mission chased him all the way to the garden of Gethsemane. Again he wrestles with temptation, causing sweat like drops of blood to pour off him. "Oh, Father, let this cup pass from me. Not this."

Even when Jesus is hanging on the cross and people go past him and they're jeering him, what are they doing? It's the same temptation. "Look at him, he saved others, he can't save himself. Why don't you come down if you're the Messiah? There's no such thing as a Messiah that comes with a cross." But Jesus stares the shadow in the face, and at a cost we will never understand, not for all eternity, he says, "No, I will suffer. I will take all of the shadow of the dark, fallen human race on myself. I will go to the cross. I will drink the cup to its last drop." He does that for us. "Not my will, but thine be done."

Without Jesus' sacrifice, without the indwelling of his Spirit, none of us would have the self-knowledge, the courage, or the strength to battle our own shadow missions. We would be as self-absorbed as Xerxes, as unsatisfied and power hungry as Haman. We would be a mere shadow of the selves God intended us to be. — John Ortberg, *Overcoming Your Shadow Mission* (Grand Rapids, MI: Zondervan, 2008).

6. **How do we keep from pursuing our shadow mission, instead of our God-given calling?**

The battle between mission and shadow mission points to a fundamental distinction between two aspects of our makeup. There is a crucial difference between giftedness and character.

By giftedness I mean talents and strengths: high IQ, athletic ability, charm, business savvy, leadership skills, charisma, good looks, popularity, artistic talent. These gifts are very good things. They all come from God. The Bible says that he is the giver of "every good and perfect gift" (James 1:17), and that we should be grateful when such gifts come our way.

But your gifts are not the most important thing about you. There is something else you have that is called character. Character is your moral and spiritual makeup; it is your habitual tendencies, the way you think and feel and intend and choose. The makeup of what is called character is what makes people trustworthy or undependable, humble or arrogant. It's a word that sounds old-fashioned—kind of Victorian—but it is not. It is who we are at the absolute core of our personhood.

Character determines our capacity to be with God, to experience God, and to know God. It determines our ability to love and relate to other people. All that is part of our character. When we are called to imitate Jesus— to be "imitators of Jesus"—we are not being called to have his giftedness or his role. Rather, we are striving for his character. — John Ortberg, *Overcoming Your Shadow Mission* (Grand Rapids, MI: Zondervan, 2008).

7. **Chapter 16. Two Cheers for Competition. What is the central idea of this chapter?**

In my business, in my marriage, in my family, in my faith, and at school, as I'm seeking to master a new discipline, I resolve to strive. Something about competition touches this resolve in us, calling it forth. War Admiral comes up and gives you the old look-in-the-eye, and you dig down deeper than you knew you could. "So long, Charley." This resolve is essential to human growth, glory, and greatness. — John Ortberg, *When the Game Is Over, It All Goes Back in the Box* (Grand Rapids, MI: Zondervan, 2008).

8. **Can competitiveness be a bad thing? When does competitiveness go bad?**

Closely allied with envy and jealousy is the spirit of competitiveness—the urge to always win or be the top person in whatever our field of endeavor is. The competitive urge begins at an early age. Young children can become quite upset or angry when they don't win a simple children's game. But it isn't just children who have a problem. I've seen grown men who were in other respects exemplary Christians lose their temper when they lost or their son's team lost a ball game. Competitiveness is basically an expression of selfishness. It's the urge to win at someone else's expense. It is certainly not loving our neighbor as ourselves.

I realize I'm questioning a "sacred cow" in our culture, because we have elevated competitiveness to a virtue. We teach children directly and by example that it is good to be competitive, that this is the way one gets ahead in the world.

I question, however, whether a competitive spirit is a Christian virtue. I believe the scriptural emphasis is on the virtue of doing one's best (see, for example, 2 Timothy 2:15). In our work, we are to work heartily (see Colossians 3:23), which is another way of saying, "Do your best." But, of course, "our best" is not the same for everyone. Some have been blessed with greater skills or intelligence or spiritual giftedness. And of course always seeking to do our best should be motivated by a desire to glorify God, not win recognition for ourselves. The recognition may come, but it should not be our motivation.

Therefore, Ben the car salesman should concentrate on doing his best to sell cars in a God-honoring way. If his best makes him the top salesman in the dealership, he should not be proud but grateful to God for giving him the ability. If his best puts him third or fourth or whatever in the ranking of salesmen, he can take solace in the fact that he did his best.

Someone may argue that Paul tacitly endorsed competitiveness in 1 Corinthians 9:24: "Do you not know that in a race all the runners compete, but only one receives the prize? So run that you may obtain it." But the analogy breaks down at the point of the prize. In a race, only one runner wins and receives the prize. But in the Christian life, we may all receive the prize. Paul is not urging us to compete with one another. Rather, he is saying, "Run the Christian race with the same intensity that the runners run who are competing for the one prize."

Let me clarify that I'm not writing against friendly competition but against the competitive spirit that always has to win or be the best. Actually, I believe that healthy competition is good, especially for children and high schoolers, as it can provide an arena in which they can seek to do their best. And this kind of competition is not limited to sports. There is competition at science fairs or among bands or at spelling bees. But in whatever competition, the question the child or teenager and their parents should ask is not "Did we win?" but "Did we do our best?"

You can see now that there is a close relationship between envy, jealousy, and competitiveness. We tend to envy a peer who is ahead of us in an area we value highly. We become jealous of a person who is overtaking us. And both of these foster a competitive spirit that says, "I must always win or be number one." All of these attitudes are the result of ungodly selfishness, of thinking only of ourselves. — Jerry Bridges, *Respectable Sins: Confronting the Sins We Tolerate* (Colorado Springs, CO: NavPress, 2007), 153–155.

9. 1 Corinthians 9.24 - 27. What can sports teach us about Christian living?

A key to living above your circumstances is leaning on the faithfulness of Christ while refusing to be caught up in the instability of your surroundings. Paul used the analogy of a runner to explain how you are to respond to life's circumstances (1 Cor. 9:24–26).

You are to fix your gaze on the finish line and race with all your might toward that goal. Once God places a goal in your heart, never give up. Instead, move toward it with swiftness and courage.

Paul's goal was to take the gospel message to Asia. Three completed missionary journeys proved he had a plan and purpose. Personal testimonies bear witness that he achieved his goal, but not without cost. No one completes the race of life without facing many trials and tribulations.

Paul had a wonderful system for bypassing negative thinking and potential defeat. He looked beyond his circumstances to the sovereignty of God. He focused on the positive results of his ministry, not the personal pain.

In the end, the trials of Paul matured and strengthened his spiritual walk. Even though you are hard-pressed on every side, Jesus will bring light to all you are facing. Trust Him, and you will see His victory. — Charles F. Stanley (personal) and Charles Stanley, *I Lift up My Soul: Devotions to Start Your Day with God* (Nashville: Thomas Nelson, 2010).

10. 1 Corinthians 9.25 Strict training. What is the spiritual lesson for us in this verse?

All athletes need to go through this, but most would probably rather skip it if it were possible. It's probably the part of sports that is the least fun. Yet this is also the part that separates average athletes from top athletes.

Have you figured it out yet? It's training. Athletic training involves many different things. Proper eating, weight training and practicing are all necessary in order to get into top playing condition.

As Christians, we need to be training ourselves spiritually. This involves getting sin out of our lives and removing those things that may not be sin but are a hindrance in our respective walks with Christ. An example of this is when sports in your life begin to take away from time that you need to be devoting to God.

Paul tells us in 1 Corinthians 9:27 that he trains spiritually so that he does not become disqualified for the prize. If a person comes into a game when he hasn't been practicing or is out of shape, he is not qualified to play. He will not reach his potential.

The same is true in our spiritual lives: We need to continually bring ourselves under God's command so that we remain qualified for what He has for us. We need to be like Paul and press on toward the prize. — Jay Beard / Fellowship Of Christian Athletes and Matt Stover, *Heart of an Athlete: Daily Devotions for Peak Performance* (Grand Rapids, MI: Revell, 2006).

11. An athlete must be disciplined in order to win. What is the lesson for us?

An athlete must be disciplined if he is to win the prize. Discipline means giving up the good and the better for the best. The athlete must watch his diet as well as his hours. He must smile and say "No, thank you" when people offer him fattening desserts or invite him to late-night parties. There is nothing wrong with food or fun, but if they interfere with your highest goals, then they are hindrances and not helps. — Warren W. Wiersbe, *The Bible Exposition Commentary, vol. 1* (Wheaton, IL: Victor Books, 1996), 602.

12. Does this mean we need to try really hard to get to Heaven?

The Christian does not run the race in order to get to heaven. He is in the race because he has been saved through faith in Jesus Christ. Only Greek citizens were allowed to participate in the games, and they had to obey the rules both in their training and in their performing. Any contestant found breaking the training rules was automatically disqualified. — Warren W. Wiersbe, *The Bible Exposition Commentary, vol. 1* (Wheaton, IL: Victor Books, 1996), 602.

13. Verse 27. I strike a blow to my body. What is that talking about?

Third, he declared his determination to beat his body (literally, to give himself a "black eye"). Paul did not mean that he actually afflicted or beat his body. He was speaking metaphorically. When boxers fight vigorously, they usually end up with bruises. Paul probably meant that he followed Christ so vigorously that it sometimes caused him physical harm, such as being lashed, beaten with rods, stoned, and shipwrecked (2 Cor. 11:24–25). — Richard L. Pratt Jr, *I & II Corinthians, vol. 7, Holman New Testament Commentary* (Nashville, TN: Broadman & Holman Publishers, 2000), 152.

14. Hebrews 12.1 – 3. What do we learn about Christian living from this passage? Look for something you have never noticed before.

Players on Mike Singletary's team will not have to be the smartest or the most athletic. However, if they are going to see much action, they will need to know the fundamentals and be disciplined.

Living a successful Christian life is similar. We need to submit to the disciplines of our faith. We should construct a well-disciplined biblical plan and be consistent in fulfilling the plan. If we take these steps, we will ultimately lead successful lives.

We are not required to live spectacular lives, but we are called upon to "run with endurance."[1] This means that we must hang in there. We do not need to attempt great feats for God. We only need to lead righteous lives and consistently apply the basic principles, specifically obedience and perseverance. — Mike Singletary and Jay Carty, *Mike Singletary One-on-One* (Grand Rapids, MI: Revell, 2005).

15. "Goal" is not mentioned in this passage, as it was in the passage before. Is it suggested?

In the Christian life, we have a goal. Christians are not people who stroll along the byways of life in a completely unconcerned manner; they travel on the high road. They are not tourists, who return each night to the place from which they started; they are pilgrims who are always travelling on the way. The goal is nothing less than the likeness of Christ. The Christian life is going somewhere, and at each day's ending we would do well to ask ourselves: 'Am I any further on?' — William Barclay, *The Letter to the Hebrews, The New Daily Study Bible* (Louisville, KY; London: Westminster John Knox Press, 2002), 202.

16. Are the words discipline and disciple related? What do we learn from this?

Discipline comes from the Latin word "disco." It has nothing to do with John Travolta or the '70s dance craze; rather, it means "to learn" or "get to know something or someone."[2] It refers to the process of learning a way of life.

A disciple is an apprentice who absorbs lessons from a master. The master has learned the discipline and he passes it on to his disciple until the learner can imitate or live like the master. Such learning requires a relationship.

To be like Jesus, we must have a relationship with Him. — Mike Singletary and Jay Carty, *Mike Singletary One-on-One* (Grand Rapids, MI: Revell, 2005).

17. Who is the cloud of witnesses in Hebrews 12.1?

What a great image. Running the race —living the life — that God has set before us. And doing so before a great cloud of witnesses, those family and friends who have gone on before us and who are watching with pride as we run.

It's not easy, this race. They know it because they went before us, often being the trailblazers, the teachers.

The author of Hebrews uses the imagery of a great stadium, with the grandstands filled to capacity with the great spiritual athletes of the past, a great cloud of witnesses encouraging us through the testimonies of their lives as we take our places in the arena as followers of Christ.

They're all there —Noah, Abraham, and Enoch. Isaac, Jacob, Joseph, and Moses. People who not only crossed the finish line but provided encouragement and hope for us in the stories of their faithfulness. — Tony Dungy and Nathan Whitaker, *Building Your Team* (Carol Stream, IL: Tyndale House Publishers, Inc., 2014).

18. Imagine Noah, Abraham, and Moses watching you. How does that motivate you?

In the Christian life, we have an inspiration. We have the thought of the unseen cloud of witnesses; and they are witnesses in a double sense, for they have witnessed their confession to Christ and they are now witnesses of our performance. Christians are like runners in some crowded stadium. As they press on, the crowd looks down; and the crowd looking down are those who have already won the crown.

The first-century writer Pseudo-Longinus, in his great work On the Sublime, has a recipe for greatness in literary endeavour. 'It is a good thing', he writes, 'to form the question in our souls, "How would Homer perhaps have said this? How would Plato or Demosthenes have lifted it up to sublimity? How would Thucydides have put it in his history?" For when the faces of these people come before us in our emulation, they will, as it were, illumine our road and will lift us up to those standards of perfection which we have imagined in our minds. It would be still better if we were to suggest this to our minds, "What would this that I have said sound like to Homer, if he were standing by, or to Demosthenes, or how would they have reacted to it?" In truth it is a supreme test to imagine such a judgment court and theatre for our own private productions, and, in imagination, to submit an account of our writings to such heroes as judges.'

Actors would act with increased intensity if they knew that one of the greatest of their profession was sitting in the stalls watching them. Athletes would double their efforts if they knew that the stadium was full of famous Olympic athletes watching their performance. It is of the very essence of the Christian life that it is lived in the gaze of the heroes of the faith who lived, suffered and died in their day and generation. How can anyone avoid the struggle for greatness when an audience like that is looking down on us? — William Barclay, *The Letter to the Hebrews, The New Daily Study Bible* (Louisville, KY; London: Westminster John Knox Press, 2002), 202–203.

19. Throw off everything that hinders. What would be an example?

In the Christian life, we have a handicap. If we are encircled by the greatness of the past, we are also encircled by the handicap of our own sin. No one would attempt to climb Mount Everest weighed down with a whole load of unnecessary baggage. If we want to travel far, we must travel light. There is in life an essential duty to discard things. There may be habits, pleasures, self-indulgences or associations which hold us back. We must shed them as athletes take off their tracksuits when they go to the starting blocks; and often we will need the help of Christ to enable us to do so. — William Barclay, *The Letter to the Hebrews, The New Daily Study Bible* (Louisville, KY; London: Westminster John Knox Press, 2002), 203.

20. What do you want to remember and apply from today's conversation?

21. How can we pray for each other this week?

When the Game is Over, Lesson #8
Chapters 17 – 19
More Will Never Be Enough
Winning Alone Is Called Losing
Be the Kind of Player People Want to Sit Next To
Good Questions Have Groups Talking
www.joshhunt.com

OPEN:

Would you consider yourself more of an introvert, or extrovert?

DIG

1. **Ecclesiastes 2.1 – 10. Solomon had access to every pleasure imaginable. What did he learn?**

   Forward into the second chapter of Ecclesiastes comes the weary king, prolonging his quest for meaning. Education proved fruitless, but perhaps he'll find what he seeks in reckless abandon. These verses sound like a report from one of our tabloids or celebrity magazines.

   Solomon began with amusement: "Come now, I will test you with mirth" (Ecclesiastes 2:1). You can almost visualize the scene. His palace in Jerusalem probably resembled a tenth-century-BC version of Caesar's Palace in Las Vegas—bright lights, big city, bells and baubles everywhere. But no meaning ... no peace ... no happiness. The mornings-after all looked the same.

The possibilities for sensual pleasure were nearly endless in Solomon's world. And who had better access to those possibilities than the king? He had a palace and all its servants at his fingertips. He had rooms full of wives and concubines. And still he found no fullness. The emptiness of it brought him to a wise realization: "Even in laughter the heart may sorrow, and the end of mirth may be grief" (Proverbs 14:13). For many, laughter only breaks the monotony of crying, and pleasure is only an intermission to pain. Solomon was trying to be happy, but he was failing.

So many today can empathize with Solomon. They've been down the road of pleasure and found that it led nowhere but to destruction. — David Jeremiah, *Searching for Heaven on Earth: How to Find What Really Matters in Life* (Nashville, TN: Thomas Nelson Publishers, 2004), 25–26.

2. Why wasn't Solomon happy? What is the lesson for us?

Solomon specifically mentioned wine and laughter as two sources of pleasure used in his experiment. It takes very little imagination to see the king in his splendid banquet hall (1 Kings 10:21), eating choice food (1 Kings 4:22–23), drinking the very best wine, and watching the most gifted entertainers (2:8b). But when the party was over and King Solomon examined his heart, it was still dissatisfied and empty. Pleasure and mirth were only vanity, so many soap bubbles that quickly burst and left nothing behind. — Warren W. Wiersbe, *Be Satisfied,*

"Be" Commentary Series (Wheaton, IL: Victor Books, 1996), 34.

3. **Pleasure can make a good dessert, but a poor entre. Why is this?**

Today's world is pleasure-mad. Millions of people will pay almost any amount of money to "buy experiences" and temporarily escape the burdens of life. While there is nothing wrong with innocent fun, the person who builds his or her life only on seeking pleasure is bound to be disappointed in the end.

Why? For one thing, pleasure-seeking usually becomes a selfish endeavor; and selfishness destroys true joy. People who live for pleasure often exploit others to get what they want, and they end up with broken relationships as well as empty hearts. People are more important than things and thrills. We are to be channels, not reservoirs; the greatest joy comes when we share God's pleasures with others.

If you live for pleasure alone, enjoyment will decrease unless the intensity of the pleasure increases. Then you reach a point of diminishing returns when there is little or no enjoyment at all, only bondage. For example, the more that people drink, the less enjoyment they get out of it. This means they must have more drinks and stronger drinks in order to have pleasure; the sad result is desire without satisfaction. Instead of alcohol, substitute drugs, gambling, sex, money, fame, or any other pursuit, and the principle will hold true: when pleasure alone is the center of life, the result will ultimately be disappointment and emptiness. — Warren W. Wiersbe, *Be Satisfied, "Be" Commentary Series* (Wheaton, IL: Victor Books, 1996), 34–35.

4. What is the difference between entertainment and enjoyment?

There is a third reason why pleasure alone can never bring satisfaction: it appeals to only part of the person and ignores the total being. This is the major difference between shallow "entertainment" and true "enjoyment," for when the whole person is involved, there will be both enjoyment and enrichment. Entertainment has its place, but we must keep in mind that it only helps us to escape life temporarily. True pleasure not only brings delight, but it also builds character by enriching the total person. — Warren W. Wiersbe, *Be Satisfied, "Be" Commentary Series* (Wheaton, IL: Victor Books, 1996), 35.

5. Ortberg talks about the "hedonic treadmill." What does he mean by that?

Eckert also said that when we get those things we thought would make us happy, we are happy, until we're not. I love that statement. She shares that psychologists call this the "hedonic treadmill," in which the efficacy of a new pleasure wears off over time. The more feel-good stuff we do or have, the more we need in order to achieve the same level of happiness.6 It's like the tolerance that develops over time in addictions, so we need three of something now instead of the two that once satisfied us. — Joyce Meyer, *The Mind Connection: How the Thoughts You Choose Affect Your Mood, Behavior, and Decisions* (New York City, NY: FaithWords, 2015).

6. Ortberg says, "Materialism is for most of us God's main rival." Do you agree?

In our day there is no anti-theism as formidable as materialism. — Conrad Emil Lindberg, *Apologetics or A*

System of Christian Evidence, Lutheran Seminary Text Book Series (Rock Island, IL: Augustana Book Concern, 1917), 50.

7. What is materialism? How would you define it?

Answer: Materialism is defined as "the preoccupation with material things rather than intellectual or spiritual things." If a Christian is preoccupied with material things, it is definitely wrong. That is not to say we cannot have material things, but the obsession with acquiring and caring for "stuff" is a dangerous thing for the Christian, for two reasons.

First, any preoccupation, obsession or fascination with anything other than God is sinful and is displeasing to God. We are to "love the Lord, your God, with all your heart, and with all your soul, and with all your might" (Deuteronomy 6:5), which is, according to Jesus, the first and greatest commandment (Matthew 22:37-38). Therefore, God is the only thing we can (and should) occupy ourselves with habitually. He alone is worthy of our complete attention, love and service. To offer these things to anything, or anyone, else is idolatry.

Second, when we concern ourselves with the material world, we are easily drawn in by the "deceitfulness of wealth" (Mark 4:19), thinking that we will be happy or fulfilled or content if only we had more of whatever it is we are chasing. This is a lie from the father of lies, Satan. He wants us to be chasing after something he knows will never satisfy us so we will be kept from pursuing that which is the only thing that can satisfy— God Himself. Luke 16:13 tells us we "cannot serve both God and money." We must seek to be content with what we have, and materialism is the exact opposite of that contentment. It causes us to strive for more and more and more, all the while telling us that this will be the answer to all our needs and dreams. The Bible tells us that a person's "life is not in the abundance of the things which he possesses" (Luke 12:15) and that we are to "seek first the kingdom of God and His righteousness" (Matthew 6:33).

If materialism was ever to satisfy anyone, it would have been Solomon, the richest king the world has ever known. He had absolutely everything and had more of it than anyone, and yet he found it was all worthless and futile. It did not produce happiness or the satisfaction our souls long for. He declared, "Whoever loves money never has money enough; whoever loves wealth is never satisfied with his income" (Ecclesiastes 5:10). In the end, Solomon came to the conclusion that we are to "fear God, and keep His commandments. For this is the whole duty of man" (Ecclesiastes 12:13). https://www.gotquestions.org/materialism-Christian.html

8. How can we get over the tendency to want more, more, more?

Have you ever opened your refrigerator, stared inside at all of the hundreds of food items, and then declared, "There's nothing to eat!" Might sound like a silly example, but that's often how it is when we forget to be grateful for what we have. We don't always remember that God is supernaturally supplying our every need. We're loaded with good things—a home to live in, a car to drive, friends to share the load, a decent job—and yet we feel like we're lacking. We want more.

More isn't really a bad thing, but when you're fixated on wishing, hoping, dreaming for more, more, more, it can drive you to be discontent, and discontentment is the enemy of peace. Truth is, God promises to meet your needs. And He does! That's not to say He won't lavish you abundantly, above all you could ask or think. He adores you and delights in bringing a smile to your face and by blessing you unexpectedly. But discontentment, grumbling, constantly striving for more, more, more... well, these things will distract you from where you need to be.

The next time you open your refrigerator, pause for a moment and thank God for what He has already supplied. Ask Him to give you that same sense of satisfaction about your home, your wardrobe, your job. And remember, God cares more about you than He does all of the rest of nature. If He clothes the birds, if He tends to the animals in the field, supplying their every need...won't He do even more for you, His child?

God will provide. He will. We still work. We still have wants and wishes, but ultimately, every good thing comes from above. Don't believe it? Ask Andrea. She and her husband lived a simple life. Their house wasn't large. Their car often needed work. But she diligently praised God for every blessing. Every time an unexpected check came in, every time an appliance lasted longer than she expected, she praised Him. Instead of craving more, more, more, she settled the issue in her heart and expressed gratitude for what was right in front of her. As a result, the Lord gave her more. Andrea's husband got an offer of a job and they ended up moving to a new home in another city. A bigger home. Not that it really mattered to Andrea. She'd been perfectly content in the old home.

Can you relate to her story, or are you constantly striving for more? Today, why not pause and thank God for meeting your every need. If He chooses to bless you above and beyond what you need, then praise Him all over again! — J. A. Thompson and Janice Hanna,

From God's Word to a Woman's Heart: A Devotional
(Uhrichsville, OH: Barbour, 2014).

9. **Chapter 18. Winning Alone Is Called Losing. Ortberg begins this chapter with the touching story of Jake Porter. Who can recall this story?**

When seventeen-year-old Jake Porter ran onto the football field, both teams cheered. Odd that they would. In three years on the Northwest High squad, he'd barely dirtied a game jersey. The McDermott, Ohio, fans had never seen Jake carry the ball or make a tackle. Nor had they seen him read a book or write much more than a sentence. Kids with chromosomal fragile X syndrome, a common cause of mental retardation, seldom do.

But Jake loved sports. Each day after his special-ed classes, he dashed off to some practice: track, baseball, basketball. Never missed. Never played, either.

Until the Waverly game.

Jake's coach made his decision before the kickoff. If a lopsided score rendered the final seconds superfluous, Jake would come in. The lopsided part proved true. With five ticks remaining on the clock, his team was down 42–0. So the coach called a time-out.

He motioned to speak with the opposing coach. As his Waverly counterpart heard the plan, he began shaking his head and waving his hands. He disagreed with something. A referee intervened, and play resumed.

The quarterback took the ball and handed it to Jake. Jake knew what do: take a knee and let the clock expire. They'd practiced this play all week. But, to his surprise, the players wouldn't let him. His teammates told him to run. So he did. In the wrong direction. So the back judge stopped and turned him around.

That's when the Waverly defense did their part. The visiting coach, as it turns out, wasn't objecting to the play. He was happy for Porter to carry the ball but not for him just to run out the clock. He wanted Jake to score. Waverly players parted like the Red Sea for Moses and shouted for Jake to run. Run he did. Grinning and dancing and jumping all the way to the end zone.

Both sidelines celebrated. Moms cried, cheerleaders whooped, and Jake smiled as if he'd won the lottery without buying a ticket. — Max Lucado, *Come Thirsty* (Nashville, TN: W Pub. Group, 2004), 107–108.

10. What is the lesson for us in this story?

The greatest joy in life is bringing others joy—especially to those on the bottom.

11. 1 Corinthians 13.1 – 3. What do we learn about love from this passage? How would you summarize it?

Love is more valuable than oratory. Love is more valuable than prophecy. Love is more valuable than knowledge. Love is more valuable even that faith. Look at it in verse 2: He says, "and though I have all faith … and have not [love], I am nothing" (1 Corinthians 13:2). Now, faith is important. You can't get to Heaven without trusting the Lord, but what he's saying is this: What good is it if you have faith so that you can remove mountains, and you can't remove malice? If your heart is headquarters for hate … Then, he says, "You are a zero. You're nothing." — Adrian Rogers, "Learning to Love," in *Adrian Rogers Sermon Archive* (Signal Hill, CA: Rogers Family Trust, 2017), 1 Co 13.

12. Make love a priority. Make relationships a priority. Make people a priority. I think we all know that. How do we make it a priority?

I believe the most important word in the English language, apart from proper nouns, is relationship. You say, "But love has to be the most important word."

I ask you, though, where is love going to be if there is no relationship? Relationship is the track. Love is what rolls over the track. Love moves through a relationship. But the thing that satisfies the deepest longing of your being is a relationship with someone.

You may think you want to be a Henry David Thoreau and go to a secluded Walden Pond to get away from the world. But Thoreau did not stay there forever and neither could you. Why? There is something in the nature of people—something built into people—that desires to be wanted, to be needed, to be fulfilled. Those desires are fulfilled only in relationships.

In the relationships of life, we must have an inner relationship. We cannot go off somewhere by ourselves. However, if we cannot get along with people, going off by ourselves may seem best. But we will not be fulfilled because something in our nature cries out for fellowship.

Rare is the individual who wants to be a loner. In being a loner, a person loses the purpose for existence because God wants to reveal his character through a Christian's life. He does this by loving through you in your relationships with others.

John said, "What we have seen and heard we proclaim to you also, that you also may have fellowship with us; and indeed our fellowship is with the Father, and with

His Son Jesus Christ" (1 John 1:3). — Carolyn T. Ritzman, Claude King, and W. Oscar Thompson, *Concentric Circles of Concern: From Self to Others through Life-Style Evangelism* (Nashville: B&H, 1999).

13. When you think of the joy of relationships, what pictures come to mind?

Consider all of the warm wonderful times of joy and happiness. Do you remember:

- The warm caress of your parents' hands;

- The giggles and laughter as you romped with your friends or brothers and sisters in the bright sunshine of a summer afternoon;

- The joy of your first date with that bright-eyed boy or girl;

- The look of enthusiasm in those with whom you work?

All these relationships make you what you are. Right relationships with parents leave you mentally and emotionally ready for marriage or for a baby brought into the family—new relationships. The special days of happiness—birthday, anniversary, Thanksgiving, Christmas—are fulfilling because of warm, wonderful relationships. Right relationships allow you to experience the best life has to offer. — Carolyn T. Ritzman, Claude King, and W. Oscar Thompson, *Concentric Circles of Concern: From Self to Others through Life-Style Evangelism* (Nashville: B&H, 1999).

14. When you think of the pain of broken relationships, what pictures come to mind?

A little more reflection about the importance of relationships will lead to some more obvious but amazing conclusions. Think about the crisis times of your life:

- As a child separated from your parents;

- As a child angry with your parents;

- As a teenager breaking up with your sweetheart;

- The resentment and misunderstanding that separated you from a friend;

- Perhaps the loss of a parent or spouse—remember the emptiness, the heartbreak;

- An argument with your husband or wife—maybe even divorce;

- A crisis with an employee or employer;

- Times of resentment and rupture with family;

- The distress in business or in your church.

List all the dark, sad, unhappy times in your life, and you will see that the vast majority of these times was created by ruptured, strained, or broken relationships. — Carolyn T. Ritzman, Claude King, and W. Oscar Thompson, *Concentric Circles of Concern: From Self to Others through Life-Style Evangelism* (Nashville: B&H, 1999).

15. The theme of love continues in Chapter 19: Be the Kind of Player People Want to Sit Next To. Among other things, Ortberg discusses some things that

kill relationships. What are some examples. (Feel free to peek.)

Forgiveness is really about healing relationships. Our relationship with God was permanently damaged because of sin. Since the wages of sin is death, Christ paid those wages for us, and He forgave us. It's done. Over with. In the past. Now our relationship with God can be fully restored.

Every day, we're given opportunities to model forgiveness. People hurt us, and our relationships are damaged. Often, we hurt others without intending to do so. Even when we're intentionally cruel, we usually don't understand the full scope of our actions. When we consider how much God has forgiven us, and how He fully restored our relationship to Him despite all the pain we caused Him, we see our own hurts in a new light. If He forgave us for rejecting Him, why wouldn't we forgive those around us?

Just as God wanted to heal the broken relationship with us, He wants us to promote healing in our relationships with each other. That's why forgiveness is so important to Him. He forgave us, and He wants us to forgive one another. Forgiveness is the key to healing in relationships, for us and for the person we forgive. — Renae Brumbaugh et al., *One-a Daily Devotional: One Way, One Truth, One Life* (Uhrichsville, OH: Barbour, 2015).

16. What does it cost us when we don't forgive? What does it cost us when we hang on to a grudge?

The embers of a grudge require tending. Resentment left to itself flickers and dies out. It must be fed to be kept alive. Where does this fuel come from? It comes from your own mental and emotional energies. Carrying

a grudge pokes holes in your energy bucket. You will feel constantly tired, weary, and lethargic. Fatigue is the faithful companion of a grudge. At the end of each day you will collapse in exhaustion, wondering why you feel so fatigued. It is because you are wasting great amounts of unconscious energy maintaining your grudge. Releasing this grudge through forgiveness will result in a brand new surge of emotional and physical energy.
— Keith Drury, *Spiritual Disciplines for Ordinary People* (Indianapolis, IN: Wesleyan Publishing House, 2004), 55–56.

17. I have heard it said that a grudge is like cancer. How so?

If we slow down and reflect a few moments, each of us will come to admit that a grudge is an awful blot on our soul. What do we gain? Why not release our grudge now? Have you been hurt deeply? Ever? By whom? Has this personal injustice ignited resentment in your heart? Has your resentment turned into a grudge? If so, think about these consequences of a grudge.

Grudges Don't Work

When someone hurts us, we are inclined to settle the score, get even. If we do not forgive the offender, the choice remaining is to try revenge, or decide to hold a grudge. Revenge is an outward attempt to even the score. A grudge is revenge turned inward. But a grudge doesn't work. The person who hurt us may not even know how angry and bitter we feel. In fact, they may go on their merry way, completely oblivious to our feelings of resentment. They are happy. We are angry, sour, and bitter. The irony: in getting even with another, we hurt ourselves—spiritually, emotionally, and perhaps even physically.

A Grudge Grows like Cancer

Inner resentment is a spreading cancer of the soul.
It multiplies its malignant tentacles, spreading to the
deepest parts of our heart. A grudge pours its corrosive
bitterness into our entire mindset. Soon we open the
door for envy, malice, jealousy, bitterness, gossip, and
slander. We will stop at nothing to even the score.
Holding a grudge will eat at your insides. Eventually you
will become a bitter person. All this happens because
you refuse to forgive the one who hurt you. The price
is too high. It's not worth it. — Keith Drury, *Spiritual
Disciplines for Ordinary People* (Indianapolis, IN:
Wesleyan Publishing House, 2004), 53–54.

18. How do we forgive when it is hard to forgive?

Have you been hurt? Has someone been unjust to you?
A parent? Brother or sister? Child? Neighbor? Teacher?
Former spouse? Perhaps you've been hurt by a group or
institution: a school, church, committee, board, or youth
group. Have you fully forgiven these people? Do you
harbor a bit of a grudge for anyone anywhere in your
past?

If so, you can get this monkey off your back for good
today! You can decide that from this hour forward, you
are marking the debt "paid in full." It is in the decision
to forgive that you can actually forgive. You can do it.
You can! In one single transaction, you can determine
that you will no longer consider that your offender has
an "outstanding balance" with you. The debt is history,
cancelled, paid in full, turned over to the Eternal Debt
Collector—not because they were right, but simply
because you want to obey Christ and please the Father.
He has commanded that you forgive others as His
Father forgave you. How was that? Completely, wholly,
irrevocably. Can you do the same for another now? It's

not a question of who's right; it's a question of what's right.

Perhaps your injury was especially deep. Could you at least begin to forgive? Are you telling yourself, "I can't forgive," when you really mean, "I won't forgive"? Are you truly unable to forgive? Are you willing to be made willing? Is the Lord gently urging you to begin? If so, why not turn the corner today? Why not tell Him right now, "Lord, I'm going to begin my road to recovery, and I shall not turn back until I have fully forgiven that person." The Great Forgiver will help you. — Keith Drury, *Spiritual Disciplines for Ordinary People* (Indianapolis, IN: Wesleyan Publishing House, 2004), 58–59.

19. What did you learn today? What insight do you want to take with you?

20. How can we pray for each other this week?

When the Game is Over, Lesson #9
Chapters 20 - 21
Collect the Right Trophies
The King Has One More Move
Good Questions Have Groups Talking
www.joshhunt.com

OPEN:

Do you have any trophies?

DIG

1. **Chapter 20. Collect the right trophies. How would you summarize the message of this chapter?**

   Jesus talked a lot about the rewards of following him. But the pursuit of rewards can break us when we go after the wrong kind. C. S. Lewis distinguished between what might be called intrinsic and extrinsic rewards. If I want to marry a woman for her money, that's seeking an extrinsic reward. It is mercenary and selfish and ultimately will be hollow. If I marry her for love, that too is a kind of reward, but it's the one that properly goes with the action. Love always seeks the enjoyment of its object. The musician who masters her instrument to win louder applause than her rivals is mercenary; the one who plays for the joy of music wins a reward that cannot be taken away.

The difference between intrinsic and extrinsic rewards is the difference between loving to learn versus wanting to have a GPA that will impress others. It's working for the joy of the craft versus working for the corner office or the envied title. It's cultivating a friendship with someone because I simply enjoy being with them versus trying to impress them because I think some of their importance or status could rub off on me.

A trophy is not the achievement itself—it's not the learning that we have gained or the muscles that we have trained or the courage we have expended. It's a symbol of achievement. It's an external validation of our worth. At best, the trophies in the case are a little reminder, something to make us grateful for the past and motivated for the future. At its worst, the trophy case becomes a shrine, a tool to prop up a false image of ourselves.

Too much of my life has been about collecting trophies. Living for trophies leaves me hollow, empty, depressed, and tired. Trophies bring a momentary pleasure that can be addicting, but the pleasure always wears off. This is why in heaven when images like "crowns" are used, people are constantly casting them at the Lord's feet. When you give glory and praise and honor away, they bring joy; when you hoard them, they tarnish and fade and become a burden. — John Ortberg, *When the Game Is Over, It All Goes Back in the Box* (Grand Rapids, MI: Zondervan, 2008).

2. **Do a search on you Bible app for the word "reward." Alternatively, do a Google search for, "Bible reward"**

(no quotes). By way of overview, what does the Bible teach about reward?

Whatever you do, work at it with all your heart, as working for the Lord, not for human masters, since you know that you will receive an inheritance from the Lord as a reward. It is the Lord Christ you are serving. Colossians 3:23-24 | NIV |

God "will repay each person according to what they have done." Romans 2:6 | NIV |

Therefore, my dear brothers and sisters, stand firm. Let nothing move you. Always give yourselves fully to the work of the Lord, because you know that your labor in the Lord is not in vain. 1 Corinthians 15:58 | NIV |

Let us not become weary in doing good, for at the proper time we will reap a harvest if we do not give up. Galatians 6:9 | NIV |

His master replied, 'Well done, good and faithful servant! You have been faithful with a few things; I will put you in charge of many things. Come and share your master's happiness!' Matthew 25:21 | NIV https://dailyverses.net/reward

3. **Philippians 4.1 Paul calls the Philippians his, "crown." What does he mean by that?**

The apostle Paul's joy came from fellow believers. Today's verse says the Philippian believers were his "joy and crown." To the Thessalonian believers he likewise proclaimed, "What is our hope, or joy, or crown of rejoicing? Is it not even you in the presence of our Lord Jesus Christ at His coming? For you are our glory and joy" (1 Thess. 2:19–20).

Paul rejoiced in the church's salvation and spiritual growth, which is represented by the word crown. The term refers to a laurel wreath, something an athlete received in biblical times for winning a contest (1 Cor. 9:25). But an athlete wasn't the only recipient of such a wreath. If someone was honored by his peers, he too would receive one as the guest of honor at a great feast or banquet. The wreath then was symbolic of success or a fruitful life. The Philippian believers were Paul's reward—proof that his efforts were successful. As you minister your gifts, may you experience the kind of joy Paul had. — John MacArthur, *Truth for Today: A Daily Touch of God's Grace* (Nashville, Tenn.: J. Countryman, 2001), 333.

4. **Complete this sentence: In the Bible, the crown is a metaphor for...**

And then there are the eternal rewards. Some of them are referred to as "crowns" that are being set aside for God's servants. The Bible speaks of at least five crowns:

The imperishable crown (1 Cor. 9:24–27), awarded to those believers who consistently bring the flesh under the Holy Spirit's control.

The crown of exultation (Phil. 4:1; 1 Thess. 2:19–20), distributed to those servants who are faithful to declare the gospel.

The crown of righteousness (2 Tim. 4:7–8), awarded to those who live each day with eternity's values in view.

The crown of life (James 1:12), promised to those who endure trials, loving the Savior all the way.

The crown of glory (1 Pet. 5:1–4), promised to those who faithfully "shepherd the flock."

What a scene! All God's servants before His throne. They are bowing in worship, having cast all crowns before their Lord in adoration and praise, ascribing worth and honor to the only One deserving of praise—the Lord God! — Charles R. Swindoll, *Day by Day with Charles Swindoll* (Nashville: Thomas Nelson, 2005).

5. Are we to serve God for the crown—the reward— we will receive?

Every Sunday morning at 11 A.M., Hebrews 11:6 enters combat with Immanuel Kant. "Without faith it is impossible to please [God], for whoever would draw near to God must believe that he exists and that he rewards those who seek him." You cannot please God if you do not come to Him for reward! Therefore, worship that pleases God is the hedonistic pursuit of God. He is our exceeding great reward! In His presence is fullness of joy, and at His right hand are pleasures forevermore. Worship is the feast of Christian Hedonism. — John Piper, *Desiring God* (Sisters, OR: Multnomah Publishers, 2003), 101–102.

6. Lewis taught we ought to have a greater desire for reward. We are too easily pleased. What did he mean by that?

If you asked twenty good men today what they thought the highest of the virtues, nineteen of them would reply, Unselfishness. But if you had asked almost any of the great Christians of old, he would have replied, Love. You see what has happened? A negative term has been substituted for a positive, and this is of more than philological importance. The negative idea of Unselfishness carries with it the suggestion not primarily of securing good things for others, but of going without them ourselves, as if our abstinence and not their happiness was the important point. I do not think this is the Christian virtue of Love. The New Testament has lots to say about self-denial, but not about self-denial as an end in itself. We are told to deny ourselves and to take up our crosses in order that we may follow Christ; and nearly every description of what we shall ultimately find if we do so contains an appeal to desire. If there lurks in most modern minds the notion that to desire our own good and earnestly to hope for the enjoyment of it is a bad thing, I submit that this notion has crept in from Kant and the Stoics and is no part of the Christian faith. Indeed, if we consider the unblushing promises of reward and the staggering nature of the rewards promised in the Gospels, it would seem that Our Lord finds our desires not too strong, but too weak. We are half-hearted creatures, fooling about with drink and sex and ambition when infinite joy is offered us, like an ignorant child who wants to go on making mud pies in a slum because he cannot imagine what is meant by the offer of a holiday at the sea. We are far too easily pleased. — C. S. Lewis, *The Weight of Glory: And Other Addresses* (New York: HarperOne, 2001), 25–26.

7. Matthew 25.21, 23. Who gets to hear, "well done" in this passage?

As the clock ticked down at the end of our Super Bowl win over the Chicago Bears in February 2007, we hugged each other. It was such a spectacular moment for the Indianapolis Colts to finally finish a season the way we had hoped. All the details we had worked on for so many months, all the way back to the off-season conditioning in February 2006. All the meetings and game preparation, all the film the coaches watched for months up until just two days earlier. The rehabilitation of injuries for so many guys. Fighting through illnesses. On and on. All of it had culminated in this celebratory moment.

"Well done." "Congratulations." "You finished what we set out to do," I told the players.

It was glorious. But it was only a fraction of what I anticipate we'll see when we finish this life and participate in the ultimate celebration.

I anticipate a scene in heaven when God tells us, "Well done, my good and faithful servants. Well done."

It was special to share that feeling of accomplishment with each other after the Super Bowl victory, but I can only imagine how spectacular it will be to hear those words from God!

But don't get me wrong—His "well done" comes in large part through grace. I can never overcome my sin and have Him say "well done" on my merits alone. I can remain faithful and stay on course as best as I can, knowing that Christ will present me to His Father as "blameless" and "without a single fault" (Colossians 1:22; Jude 1:24). I will strive to show Christ's love for me through my compassion for others and my faithfulness to Him, even though I know my attempts will always fall short.

But I will keep trying and will look forward to that glorious day—well done, indeed!

What have you celebrated recently that makes you think, It couldn't get any better than this? It certainly does. And how you live your life makes the difference.
— Tony Dungy and Nathan Whitaker, *Living Your Life's Purpose* (Carol Stream, IL: Tyndale House Publishers, Inc., 2014).

8. Revelation 22.12; Romans 2.6 – 8. Are rewards on the basis of grace or works?

Rewards are part of God's plan for His people. The Bible is filled with truth about rewards. We have been talking about the final warnings of the Lord Jesus to His people before going back to heaven as well as His final words of hope and encouragement. One of those wonderful warnings and challenges is found in Revelation 22:12 where He reminds us: "Behold, I am coming quickly, and My reward is with Me, to give every one according to his work."

THE JUDGMENT OF BELIEVERS' WORKS

Rewards are present everywhere in Scripture. Listen to some of these statements from the Word of God.

Psalm 58:11: "So that men will say, 'Surely there is a reward for the righteous; surely He is God who judges in the earth.' "

Psalm 62:12: "Also to You, O Lord, belongs mercy; for You render to each one according to his work."

Hebrews 6:10–12: "For God is not unjust to forget your work and labor of love which you have shown toward His name, in that you have ministered to the saints, and do minister. And we desire that each one of you show the same diligence to the full assurance of hope until the end, that you do not become sluggish, but imitate those who through faith and patience inherit the promises."

In the New Testament, the Lord Jesus constantly talked to His disciples about the importance of rewards.

Mark 10:29–30 reads, "So Jesus answered and said, 'Assuredly, I say to you, there is no one who has left house or brothers or sisters or father or mother or wife or children or lands, for My sake and the gospel's, who shall not receive a hundredfold now in this time— houses and brothers and sisters and mothers and children and lands, with persecutions—and in the age to come, eternal life.' "

Matthew 5:12 says, "Rejoice and be exceedingly glad, for great is your reward in heaven, for so they persecuted the prophets who were before you."

We cannot read the Bible without bumping into rewards at every turn. But some people inevitably come along and say, "Well, the Bible doesn't mean rewards like we think of rewards today. It means something totally different."

The word reward comes from a couple of Hebrew and Greek words, and it means "payment for something done." In the New Testament, we find a well-defined system for the day when God rewards His people. — David Jeremiah, *Until Christ Returns: Living Faithfully Today While We Wait for Our Glorious Tomorrow (Study Guide)* (Nashville, TN: Thomas Nelson Publishers, 2007), 104–105.

9. **Last Chapter. The King Has One More Move. What is the message of this chapter?**

Our longing is not just for a longer life—not even for an indefinite extension, particularly if all such an extension would mean is more of the same. A Christian college in Southern California once sent students door to door to talk with people about spiritual issues. Two of them knocked on one door to find a frenzied mother of three with a vacuum in one hand and a screaming baby in the other arm, food burning on the stove, and a living room so messy it would have qualified as a federal disaster area. "Are you interested in eternal life?" one of the students asked. "Frankly, I don't think I could stand it," said the mom.

We want more than more of the same. We want what's wrong to be put right. We want suffering to stop. We want clean air, meaningful work, honest politicians, clear consciences, ceaseless beauty, instant Internet connections, the end of loneliness and war. We want the whole enchilada. We want heaven. And what we want is in the hands of the Master of the Board and in his final move. — John Ortberg, *When the Game Is Over, It All Goes Back in the Box* (Grand Rapids, MI: Zondervan, 2008).

10. 1 Corinthians 15.55. "Death is both undesirable and inevitable, and human life hangs by a slender thread." — Ortberg. How does the resurrection (see the context of 1 Corinthians 15) change this?

Think about the holes children make when they dig in the sand on the seashore. When the waves come in, the holes are swallowed up by the ocean. Similarly, when we know Christ, our physical death is overwhelmed by the love and grace of God. Death is swallowed up in the victory of Christ.

Death is an incident, not an end. It is a transition for a Christian, not a terminus. In death, we are freed from all that burdens us here. We lay aside the outward "tent" of our body, and we inherit "a building from God, a house not made with hands, eternal in the heavens" (2 Corinthians 5:1 NASB).

Here, our lives are filled with suffering and confusion. We experience pain and problems, and sometimes life seems to have no meaning or purpose. But the resurrection of Jesus Christ changed all that. It gives purpose and meaning to life, and life's greatest joy comes from discovering His will and fulfilling it. His resurrection also gives us hope—hope right now, and hope beyond the grave. May these truths encourage you this day! — Billy Graham, *Hope for Each Day Morning and Evening Devotions* (Nashville: Thomas Nelson, 2012).

11. Psalm 116.15. How is God's perspective on death different than ours? How can we come to see things the way God sees things?

Death is the one experience through which all will pass. We may meet it with resignation, denial, or even without a moment's thought—but come it will.

But death for the believer is distinctly different from what it is for the unbeliever. For us, it isn't something to be feared or shunned, for we know death is but the shadowed threshold to the palace of God. No wonder Paul declared, "I desire to depart and be with Christ, which is better by far" (Philippians 1:23 NIV).

Sometimes God gives His departing saints glimpses of Heaven (partly, I believe, to encourage those of us who remain). Just before dying, my grandmother sat up in bed, smiled, and said, "I see Jesus, and He has His hand outstretched to me. And there is Ben, and he has both of his eyes and both of his legs." (Ben, my grandfather, had lost an eye and a leg at Gettysburg.)

Are you looking forward to that day when you will go to be with Christ, "which is better by far"? — Billy Graham, *Hope for Each Day Morning and Evening Devotions* (Nashville: Thomas Nelson, 2012).

12. John 11.25 – 26. Some say Jesus was a good, moral teacher, but not the Son of God. What did Jesus teach about Himself?

I am trying here to prevent anyone saying the really foolish thing that people often say about Him: 'I'm ready to accept Jesus as a great moral teacher, but I don't accept His claim to be God.' That is the one thing we must not say. A man who was merely a man and said the sort of things Jesus said would not be a great moral teacher. He would either be a lunatic—on a level with the man who says he is a poached egg—or else he would be the Devil of Hell. You must make your choice. Either this man was, and is, the Son of God: or else a madman or something worse. You can shut Him up for a fool, you can spit at Him and kill Him as a demon; or you can fall at His feet and call Him Lord and God. But let us not come with any patronising nonsense about His being a great human teacher. He has not left that open to us. He did not intend to. — C. S. Lewis, *Mere Christianity* (New York: HarperOne, 2001), 52.

13. Is Heaven a real, physical place?

Heaven is not a theoretical concept or a state of mind. It is not make-believe or pretend or a figment of somebody's imagination. Just like Miami and London and Tokyo are actual places, Heaven is a real and actual place. In John 14, Jesus told the disciples that He was going to prepare a "place" for them. He wasn't going to prepare a state of mind. He wasn't going to prepare a concept. No, He was going to prepare an actual place specially created for those who have a personal relationship with God.

My Father's house has many rooms; if that were not so, would I have told you that I am going there to prepare a place for you? And if I go and prepare a place for you,

I will come back and take you to be with me that you also may be where I am. You know the way to the place where I am going. (vv. 2–4)

Notice first that Jesus refers to His Father's house and that His house has many rooms in it. Second, notice that three different times in this short passage Jesus uses the word "place." The word translated "place" has been referred to as mansions in some translations, but the reference was to rooms that were added on to the patriarch's house as sons married and brought their wives to live in the extended family compound or estate. Lastly, notice that Jesus says He is coming back to get us so that we can be with Him. So, if Jesus is real and He resides in some PLACE, then we are promised to be in that place with Him. — Chip Ingram and Lance Witt, *The Real Heaven: What the Bible Actually Says* (Grand Rapids, MI: Baker Books, 2016).

14. Do our souls "sleep" until the resurrection at the rapture?

When a believer dies, his body goes in the grave and goes to sleep. But his soul does not sleep; his soul and spirit go to Paradise.

In Scripture, "falling asleep" is a softened term for the believer's death. For instance, when Paul wrote to the Thessalonian believers, he said: "I do not want you to be ignorant, brethren, concerning those who have fallen asleep, lest you sorrow as others who have no hope" (1 Thessalonians 4:13). Paul wasn't talking about falling asleep the way we fall asleep at night. He was describing the death of Christians.

In the New Testament, the Greek word translated "to fall asleep" is koimao, which comes from the same Greek root as "to lie down." Koimao was also used to describe someone who slept in a hotel for one night and the next day would get up to continue his or her journey. This is a beautiful image of what happens to believers' bodies when they die. Their bodies go to sleep, awaiting the Resurrection at the Rapture—while their souls and spirits go to be with our Lord in heaven. — David Jeremiah, Answers to Your Questions about Heaven (Carol Stream, IL: Tyndale, 2015), 12.

15. Is there an intermediate heaven and hell?

The Bible teaches that every believer who died prior to the ascension of Christ went to an intermediate heaven called Paradise, or Abraham's bosom (Luke 16:22, KJV).

But when Jesus ascended after His death, He went into Paradise and took all who were there—all the Old Testament saints, all who had died and believed in God before the Ascension—with Him to the third heaven (Ephesians 4:8–10).

This means that believers no longer go to the intermediate heaven upon death. The souls and spirits of today's believers go immediately to the third heaven because Paradise is no longer an intermediate place; Paradise is now with God (2 Corinthians 12:2–4).

IS THERE AN INTERMEDIATE HELL? WHAT ABOUT PURGATORY?

Yes—there is an intermediate hell. When an unbeliever dies, his body goes into the grave and his spirit and soul go to Hades.

Revelation 20 tells us that "Death and Hades delivered up the dead" (verse 13). This passage indicates that Hades remains an intermediate hell until the Great White Throne Judgment—when "Death and Hades [will be] cast into the lake of fire" (verse 14)—the permanent hell.

But Hades is not a place of decision. There is no such place as purgatory. The Bible teaches that "it is appointed unto men once to die, but after this the judgment" (Hebrews 9:27, KJV).

In Luke 16:26, Abraham describes a "great gulf fixed" between Hades and Paradise, "so that those who want to pass from here to you cannot, nor can those from there pass to us." This passage illustrates the permanence of the gulf between heaven and hell. We won't be able to "cross" from one side to the other.

Whatever decisions we make about eternity will be made in this life. — David Jeremiah, *Answers to Your Questions about Heaven* (Carol Stream, IL: Tyndale, 2015), 14–15.

16. Will Heaven be boring?

Be assured that we are not going to sit idly in heaven.

What is God going to say to us when we get to heaven? I don't think He will say, "Well done, good and faithful servant; you can have the rest of eternity off." He will say, "Well done, good and faithful servant; you were faithful over a few things, I will make you ruler over many things. Enter into the joy of your lord" (Matthew 25:21). Now, that doesn't sound like we're going to be sitting around forever and ever—it sounds like there will be "many things" to do! For one, we already know that we'll be ruling and reigning with Christ over this renovated earth during the Millennium.

And Revelation 22 says, "His servants shall serve Him" (verse 3). God has a great plan for each one of us to be wonderfully, happily, excitedly employed—serving the Lord in Paradise. And we will be serving in the fullest expression of the capacity God has given us and using the giftedness He has placed within us.

What we won't experience are the difficulties, pressures, stresses, and heartaches that accompany work down here. We cannot possibly comprehend all of the glorious work with which we'll be occupied throughout eternity; but we know that our service will result in deep joy and fulfillment.

[In heaven] our minds and bodies will never fade and we will never lack resources or opportunity, [so] our work won't degenerate. Buildings won't last for only fifty years, and books won't be in print for only twenty years. They'll last forever.3 —Randy Alcorn / David Jeremiah, *Answers to Your Questions about Heaven* (Carol Stream, IL: Tyndale, 2015), 28–29.

17. Ecclesiastes 3.11. God has set eternity in our hearts. What does that mean?

Even if you know that heaven is your eternal destiny, you have probably had days when you've said, "Oh Lord, just take me home now." Do you long for the time when you never have to say good-bye again? When there will be no more sickness, no more suffering, no more growing old?

The Bible says God has set eternity in your heart. To long for a better place is not a vain hope or delusion. You were made for eternity, and because of this, you can never be fully satisfied until you get to heaven.

"Training our minds and hearts, the totality of our being on heaven, is instinctive because our souls are eternal," says Dr. Joseph Stowell. "There's something in us that feels right about believing there is something on the other side of death.

"But instincts don't quite cut it because you have to have some content. When we are born again in Jesus Christ, when we've repented of our sin, embraced the finished work of Christ on the cross, and have been reborn so that the Holy Spirit lives within us, now these instincts for eternity suddenly take on meaning because the Holy Spirit excites and nurtures our desire for home."

Let God's Spirit move inside you and excite you to live life in light of eternity.

"He has made everything beautiful in its time. He has also set eternity in the hearts of men; yet they cannot fathom what God has done from beginning to end" (Ecclesiastes 3:11). — Bill Dunn and Kathy Leonard, *Through a Season of Grief: Devotions for Your Journey from Mourning to Joy* (Nashville: Thomas Nelson, 2004).

18. Eternity in our hearts. What is the application?

I once came across a scene of beauty just a few miles outside Anchorage, Alaska, where I noticed a number of cars pulled off the highway. Whales, a pod of silvery white beluga, were feeding no more than fifty feet offshore. I stood with the other onlookers for forty minutes, listening to the rhythmic motion of the sea, following the graceful, ghostly crescents of surfacing whales. The crowd was hushed, even reverent.

The Teacher would doubtless understand the crowd's response to the whales, for he insists that though we are not gods, we are not solely animals either. God "has also set eternity in the hearts of men." Such an elegant phrase applies to much in human experience. Surely it hints at a religious instinct, an instinct that, to the bafflement of anthropologists, finds expression in every human society ever studied. Our hearts perceive eternity in ways other than religious as well. The Teacher is no nihilist; he sees with dazzling clarity the beauty in the created world.

Ecclesiastes endures as a work of great literature and a book of great truth because it presents both sides of life on this planet: the promise of pleasures so alluring that we may devote our lives to their pursuit, and then the haunting realization that these pleasures ultimately do not satisfy. God's tantalizing world is too big for us. Made for another home, made for eternity, we finally realize that nothing this side of timeless paradise will quiet the rumors of discontent.

The Teacher writes: "He has also set eternity in the hearts of men; yet they cannot fathom what God has done from beginning to end." That is the point of Ecclesiastes. The same lesson Job learned in dust and ashes—that we humans cannot figure out life on our own—the Teacher learns in a robe and palace.

Unless we acknowledge our limits and subject ourselves to God's rule, unless we trust the Giver of all good gifts, we will end up in a state of despair. Ecclesiastes calls us to accept our status as creatures under the dominion of the Creator, something few of us do without a struggle. — *The Bible Jesus Read* (157 – 60) / Philip Yancey, *Grace Notes: Daily Readings with Philip Yancey* (Grand Rapids, MI: Zondervan, 2009).

19. What did you learn in this study? What is one thing you want to remember and never forget?

20. How can we pray for each other this week?